The Jews and the Irrevocable Call of God in Reformed Theology from John Calvin to Thomas Torrance

The Jews and the Irrevocable Call of God in Reformed Theology from John Calvin to Thomas Torrance

Mark J. Larson

WIPF & STOCK · Eugene, Oregon

THE JEWS AND THE IRREVOCABLE CALL OF GOD IN REFORMED
THEOLOGY FROM JOHN CALVIN TO THOMAS TORRANCE

Wipf & Stock
An Imprint of Wipf and Stock Publishers
199 W. 8th Ave., Suite 3
Eugene, OR 97401

www.wipfandstock.com

PAPERBACK ISBN: 979-8-3852-5292-3
HARDCOVER ISBN: 979-8-3852-5293-0
EBOOK ISBN: 979-8-3852-5294-7

VERSION NUMBER 09/30/25

Unless otherwise indicated, Scripture references are from the New King
James Version. Copyright © 1982, Thomas Nelson, Inc.

Scripture references from The New American Standard Bible are identified.
Copyright © 1960, 1962, 1963, 1968, 1971, 1972, 1973, 1975, 1977, 1995,
The Lockman Foundation.

For Cynthia

Contents

Preface

SEVERAL YEARS AGO, MY wife and I were invited for dinner at the home of a pastor who had graduated from one of the Reformed theological seminaries in the United States. The subject of the Jews came up in our conversation. The pastor essentially asserted that the Jews are no longer special in the eyes of God and are no different than any other people who have heard the gospel and rejected it.[1] I was astounded by this statement coming from the mouth of a theological conservative standing in the Calvinist tradition of theology. It reminds me of what David Torrance of the Church of Scotland has contended: "There is a veil over the minds and hearts of many within the Christian Church so that they fail to understand what Scripture says about God's ongoing purpose for his covenant People."[2]

Replacement theology is even attributed to the founding fathers of the Reformed tradition. "Calvin," it has been argued, "tends to supercessionism." "He has a blind spot for the importance of the Jews."[3] One scholar maintains, "The Christian interpretation that I had learned from Reformed theologians such as John Calvin" was the position that "the covenant that God had made with Israel was transferred to those who believe in Jesus." In Calvinist theology,

---

1. Writers who advocate replacement theology include Burge, *Jesus and the Land* and Chapman, *Christian Zionism and the Restoration of Israel*.

2. Torrance and Taylor, *Israel, God's Servant*, 5.

3. Huijgen, "Calvin's Old Testament Theology and Beyond," 91.

then, "the vast majority of Jews, who had refused Jesus' claim to be Messiah, were no longer the apple of God's eye."[4]

Other students of Calvin allege that he really did not have "a clearly defined position on Israel."[5] Reference is made to "Calvin's failure to write at length on the Jews."[6] When he did write about the Jews, it is maintained that he "emphasized the anti-Jewish and toned down the pro-Jewish statements in the New Testament."[7] "Conventional anti-Jewish sentiments" are supposedly found "in Calvin's writings."[8]

In opposition to such perspectives, this study in historical theology demonstrates that John Calvin (1509–1564) had a clearly defined position on Israel and wrote at length about the Jewish people. The favor of God, he affirmed, still rests upon them. For Calvin, "the Jews should be honored on account of the station granted them by God." "That the Jews were the chosen people should not be forgotten."[9]

Wulfert de Greef properly states, "Calvin rejects the idea that the Jews have been done away with and that the Gentiles are important because they have now taken the place of the Jews." Calvin contended that "a remnant accepted Jesus as the Messiah, and Gentiles who believe in Jesus are bound together with them and with them form one people."[10] I argue in this work that not only Calvin but the major theologians of the Reformed tradition have not affirmed the fundamental tenets of replacement theology.

Calvin along with a long line of Reformed exegetes would have rejected the position that the Jews have no future other than that of castaways and expatriates, perpetual refugees upon the earth bearing witness to the judgment of God for rejecting the

4. McDermott, *Israel Matters*, xi.

5. VanGemeren, "Israel as the Hermeneutical Crux in the Interpretation of Prophecy (II)," 254.

6. Austin, *The Jews and the Reformation*, 80.

7. Baron, "John Calvin and the Jews," 387.

8. Austin, *The Jews and the Reformation*, 83,

9. Gordon, *Calvin*, 117.

10. De Greef, *Of One Tree*, 97, note 417.

Messiah Jesus and having been replaced by the church composed mainly of Gentiles, the new Israel of God. A few voices within the Reformed tradition suggest that the divine call to Israel could be revoked.[11] For Calvin and the Reformed mainstream, however, the call of God to the Jews is irrevocable.

Reformed biblical scholars over the centuries have given focused attention to the question raised by Paul in Romans 11:1 as to whether God has cast away his people Israel. It has been noted that the apostle answers with a firm negation and then declares in verse 2 that God has not cast away his people whom he foreknew. Indeed, Holy Scripture underscores the truth of Zechariah 2:8 that the one who touches Israel touches the apple of God's eye. The Calvinian tradition has been fully committed to these biblical perspectives.

This volume expands upon the scholarship of Heiko Oberman who presented an accurate and succinct summary of the teaching of Calvin on the issue of the Jews: "No longer is the New Testament presented as superseding the Old Testament." "The first among the elect are the Jews; they are the 'first born in the Church.'" The "covenant of God with the Jews" has not been replaced by "a new covenant with the Christian church." The new covenant was in fact a "renewal of the covenant with Abraham." In Calvin's reading of the New Testament, "the mission of Christ is primarily to the Jews" and "only after the resurrection is the range of the Gospel to the gentiles."[12] "Christians" in the thinking of Calvin "are *added* to the People of God and *inserted* in the Tribe of Moses." How did he regard the Old Testament? "The 'Old' or rather the 'Primary' Testament is not only Holy Scripture because of its prophetic witness to the future Messiah, but because it tells the story of God's care for his people."[13]

This author recognizes that the Reformed theological tradition did not begin with Calvin.[14] There was, as Richard Muller has

---

11. An example is Brueggemann, *Chosen? Reading the Bible amid the Israeli-Palestinian Conflict*, 17.

12. Oberman, "John Calvin: The Mystery of His Impact," 3.

13. Oberman, "John Calvin: The Mystery of His Impact," 3–4.

14. Muller, "Reception and Response," 183.

reminded us, an earlier generation of Reformed theologians—men such as Martin Bucer (1491–1551), Huldrych Zwingli (1484–1531), Wolfgang Capito (1478–1541), and Johannes Oecolampadius (1482–1531).[15] Calvin did not lay the foundation of Reformed doctrine.[16] Peter Opitz makes the declaration that "Zwingli, and not Calvin, is the founding father of Reformed Protestantism."[17] Bruce Gordon acknowledges that "Calvin inherited the Reformed tradition forged in Zurich." "Reformed Christianity came from Zurich," and it was "Zwingli" who "made the Reformation in Zurich possible."[18]

The emphasis upon Calvin's thought in this study is not based on the assumption that he created the Reformed faith.[19] The stress upon Calvin in the context of the teaching of other Reformed theologians in his time and succeeding generations is due to the fact that his teaching on the Jews and the irrevocable call of God has so often been misconstrued.[20]

It surely is a moral duty for me to give thanks to God for the wonderful biblical scholars under whom I studied in years gone by. I so appreciate Jack Riggs, Senior Professor Emeritus of Bible at Cedarville University. He ever advocated the importance of a literal hermeneutic in biblical interpretation and warned against allegorical exegesis in our handling of the Old Testament prophets. I am thankful, likewise, for John Lawlor, Emeritus Professor of Old Testament at Grand Rapids Theological Seminary. He always stressed that Jesus was a Jew and that the Scripture comes to us

---

15. Muller, "Diversity in the Reformed Tradition," 11–12.

16. Hart, *Calvinism*, 20.

17. Opitz, *Ulrich Zwingli*, 86.

18. Gordon, *Zwingli*, 7.

19. I do agree with Bard Thompson that "the greatest and most subtle mind of the Protestant Reformation belonged to John Calvin." Thompson, *Humanists and Reformers*, 471. Cf., Fesko, *Beyond Calvin*, 29; Donnelly, "Italian Influences on the Development of Calvinist Scholasticism," 81. Warfield, "Calvin and the Reformation," 401–3.

20. Richard Muller refers to "the commonalities between Calvin's own thought and that of significant numbers of predecessors and contemporaries." Muller, "Reception and Response," 182.

from the hand of the Jews.[21] Indeed, it was Paul who asked, "What advantage then has the Jew?" The apostle maintained that there was much that was given to them: "Chiefly because to them were committed the oracles of God" (Rom. 3:1–2). The Bible accordingly reflects Hebraic thought.[22]

My language professors are also remembered with gratitude—two of whom had earned their Th.D. at Grace Theological Seminary. I am referring here to George Lawlor at Cedarville University who taught me Greek and my Hebrew professor Richard Engle at Baptist Bible School of Theology. It was a blessing likewise to sit at the feet of the brilliant New Testament scholar Moisés Silva at Westminster Theological Seminary.

I am ever thankful for the opportunity given to me by God to study historical theology with Richard Muller in the doctoral program at Calvin Theological Seminary. I could not have had a better doctoral adviser. His direction and encouragement will never be forgotten. My entire approach in Calvin studies is due to his enduring influence in my life.

Let me also express my appreciation for the editors at Wipf and Stock. Their interest in this subject and their expertise in publishing quality books has made it possible for this book to be published at a time of renewed antisemitism not only in the western world but even in certain sectors of the church. It has been a pleasure to work with such courteous professionals at a premier publishing house for books in historical theology.

There are other people for whom I must give thanks as well in helping me to understand the biblical teaching on the Jews as the people loved and chosen by the Lord. There is my father who often

21. Oberman notes that Calvin embraced the "perspective of Jesus as a Jew serving the Jews." It was not until "after Pentecost" that "it is the work of the Spirit to extend the People of God and include the Gentiles." Oberman, "John Calvin: The Mystery of His Impact," 4.

22. Oberman observes, "Calvin wants it to be taken seriously that Paul was a Jew and trained as a rabbi. The Apostle writes in Greek but, as Calvin never tires of saying, he thinks 'more *hebraico*'; his writing is Greek in grammar, but Hebrew in structure and thought." Oberman, "John Calvin: The Mystery of His Impact," 4.

mentioned his belief in the ongoing validity of the statement given by God to Abraham: "I will bless those who bless you, and I will curse him who curses you" (Gen. 12:3). There is my wife Cynthia to whom this book is dedicated. She understood the central place of the Jews in the history of redemption when she first began to read through the Bible as a teenager. There is our son Daniel who is now with the Lord in the heavenly country and knows far more than his father. Indeed, he is now the real theologian in the family. I would give thanks to God for all the members of our family—my mother, our children and grandchildren, our daughter-in-law and son-in-law, my brother and his family, my two sisters-in-law and my brother-in-law. I have learned much from all of you and love you all very much.

May we all grow in our love to Christ, the Son of God, who in the incarnation became a Jew and grants the gift of eternal life to everyone who calls upon him for salvation. May we remember the prayer of Paul: "My heart's desire and prayer to God for Israel is that they may be saved" (Rom 10:1). May we recognize that the day will come when this petition will be answered. The Jews will indeed say with reference to their Messiah Jesus, "Blessed is He who comes in the name of the LORD!" (Matt 23:39).

Introduction

"GOD BY A SUDDEN conversion subdued and brought my mind to a teachable frame."[1] John Calvin here reflected upon the decisive turning point of his life using the Latin expression *subita conversione*. The adjective *subita* can mean either sudden or unexpected.[2] God intervened and changed the direction of his life. Calvin had been, he said, "too obstinately devoted to the superstitions of Popery to be so easily extricated from so profound an abyss of mire."[3] He began to submit his reason to the authority of Holy Scripture.

Jeanne le Franc, Calvin's mother, was a devout Roman Catholic who attended the shrines of the saints with the objective of lessening her time in purgatory. On one occasion the young boy made a pilgrimage with his mother to Ourscamp Abbey to kiss a holy relic, what was purported to be a piece of the body of St. Anne.[4] His father Jean Cauvin was likewise committed to the Catholic church sending his son to the University of Paris to study for the priesthood, entering first the Collège de la Marche and then the Collège de Montaigu. His father, though, suddenly changed his purpose. Calvin wrote, "It came to pass, that I was withdrawn from the study of philosophy, and was put to the study of law."[5] He thus enrolled at the University of Orléans and then Bourges to

1. Calvin, *Commentary on the Book of Psalms*, vol. 1, xl.
2. Parker, *John Calvin*, 193.
3. Calvin, *Commentary on the Book of Psalms*, vol. 1, xl.
4. Parker, *John Calvin*, 2–3.
5. Calvin, *Commentary on the Book of Psalms*, vol. 1, xl.

study law. This was the time of his unanticipated conversion.[6] He immediately turned his attention to the study of the Bible.

Mastery of the Biblical Languages

Theodore Beza (1519–1605) in his biographical account stated concerning Calvin's time of study in Orléans, "He diligently cultivated the study of sacred literature, and made such progress, that all in that city who had any desire to become acquainted with a purer religion, often called to consult him, and were greatly struck both with his learning and his zeal."[7]

In addition to his expertise in Latin, Calvin became a master of Greek and Hebrew.[8] Oberman commented, "As far as Greek is concerned, to place him in the same league as Erasmus does perhaps not do sufficient justice to his expertise." "Truly amazing," he added, "is Calvin's command of Hebrew." In fact, "the excitement of his readers and listeners to hear for the first time the Scriptures 'authentically,' usually arises from his interpretation of the Jewish Scriptures."[9]

Calvin's skill in the biblical languages presented a sharp contrast to the Sorbonne.[10] The theological faculty of the University of Paris condemned all editions of the Bible in the original languages.[11] They also regarded the Greek and Hebrew scholars who taught at the Collège Royal with suspicion because they insisted that a knowledge of the biblical languages was necessary for the accurate interpretation of Scripture.[12] Calvin rejected this

6. Parker, *John Calvin*, 195.

7. Beza, *The Life of John Calvin*, 8.

8. Zachman, "John Calvin (1509–1564)," 189.

9. Oberman, "John Calvin: The Mystery of His Impact," 3. Cf., Balserak, *Establishing the Remnant Church in France*; Engammare, "Calvin the Workaholic," 70–71; Austin, *The Jews and the Reformation*, 81; MacCulloch, "Calvin," 34.

10. Gordon, *Calvin*, 13, 32, 150.

11. Wendel, *Calvin*, 26.

12. Ganoczy, "Calvin's Life," 5; Ganoczy, "Calvin, John," 235. It is possible that Calvin had first studied Hebrew under François Vatable at the Collége Royal. De Greef, *Of One Tree*, 72.

backwoods mentality.[13] He entered the pulpit and preached from the Hebrew Bible and the Greek New Testament.[14]

There is no doubt that Calvin would have agreed with the position of the Zurich reformer Huldrych Zwingli who advocated poring over the Word of God night and day and declared, "This labour cannot be performed until one has mastered the languages of Hebrew and Greek, for without the first the Old Testament and the second the New cannot be properly understood."[15] Calvin certainly believed in the importance of vernacular translations so that "the simple common people" would be able to read the Scripture for themselves.[16] But like the German humanist Johannes Reuchlin (1455–1522), he accepted the fact that no translation was in an ultimate sense an adequate foundation for Christian doctrine.[17] "The language of the Jews," Reuchlin affirmed, "is simple, pure, uncorrupted, sacred, concise, and eternal."[18] Referring to the truth as revealed in the Hebrew Bible, Reuchlin declared, "I revere St. Jerome as an angel, and I respect Nicholas of Lyra as a great teacher, but I worship the truth as God."[19]

---

13. Cambridge University showed more sophistication than the Sorbonne appointing Paul Fagius to the chair of Hebrew in 1549. He was then succeeded by Immanuel Tremmelius, a converted Jew. Toon, *Puritans, the Millennium and the Future of Israel*, 23. John Coffey makes the point that it was "Protestant scholars" who "led the way in the rebirth of Hebrew studies in the Christian West." Coffey, *Exodus and Liberation*, 35.

14. Steinmetz, "John Calvin As an Interpreter of the Bible," 288.

15. Gordon, *Zwingli*, 99.

16. Calvin opposed what he called "the ungodly voices of some" that "are heard, shouting that it is a shameful thing to publish these divine mysteries among the simple common people." Calvin, "John Calvin's Latin Preface to Olivétan's French Bible," 374.

17. Richard Muller states that in Calvin there is an "identification of Scripture as the verbally inspired Word of God." Muller, *Post-Reformation Reformed Dogmatics*, vol. 2, 74.

18. Price, *Johannes Reuchlin*, 59; De Greef, *Of One Tree*, 43.

19. Price, *Johannes Reuchlin*, 61. Price provides Reuchlin's statement in Latin: "Quanquam enim Hieronymum sanctum veneror ut angelum et Lyram colo ut magistrum, tamen adoro veritatem ut deum" (*Johannes Reuchlin*, 248).

Biblical Commentary

Calvin determined to fulfill the call of God upon his life as a pastor and teacher by setting forth a biblical theology in two tracks—in his running expositions of the biblical text in commentaries and sermons and in his *Institutes of the Christian Religion*.[20] The latter would be the place to find doctrinal disputations and common topics—that is, topics that frequently appear throughout the Scripture (such doctrines as God, man, law, faith, repentance, justification, providence, predestination, etc.). His commentaries and sermons would be the place where he would provide more thorough expositions of the biblical text.[21]

The Preface to the 1541 French edition of the *Institutes* presents Calvin's theological project. "The present book," he said, was intended to set forth "the principal and weightiest themes which go to make up Christian philosophy."[22] "It can serve as a key and opening, allowing all of God's children access to a true and proper understanding of holy Scripture."[23] His next statements indicate that Calvin believed, as Richard Muller has indicated, that his "central task" was "that of biblical commentator."[24] "In the future, therefore," noted Calvin, "if the Lord gives me the means and opportunity to write commentaries, I will be as brief as possible. There will be no need for lengthy digressions, since I have here provided a detailed explanation of almost all the articles which concern the Christian faith."[25]

In the ensuing years, Calvin wrote commentaries on every book in the New Testament with the exception of 2 and 3 John and Revelation. He likewise produced commentaries on the

20. Muller, *The Unaccommodated Calvin*, 106. Cf., Cottret, *Calvin: A Biography*, 288–89.

21. Blacketer, "Calvin As Commentator on the Mosaic Harmony and Joshua," 32; Steinmetz, "John Calvin As an Interpreter of the Bible," 290–91.

22. Calvin, *Institutes of the Christian Religion*, 1541 edition, xv.

23. Calvin, *Institutes of the Christian Religion*, 1541 edition, xvi.

24. Muller, *The Unaccommodated Calvin*, 16. Cf., Benedict, *Christ's Churches Purely Reformed*, 82.

25. Calvin, *Institutes of the Christian Religion*, 1541 edition, xvi.

INTRODUCTION

Pentateuch, Isaiah, Psalms, and Joshua.[26] His lectures delivered without notes on all the other prophetic books of the Old Testament were also published having been recorded by a team of three secretaries.[27] Large numbers of students gathered for Calvin's lectures on the prophets. It was common, for example, for more than one thousand people to gather in the lecture hall called the *Auditoire* to hear Calvin's expositions on Jeremiah.[28]

There is no question that the central place in Calvin's writing was given to the development of biblical commentaries.[29] We must not forget, however, that the main responsibility of Calvin in Geneva focused upon preaching, the ongoing public exposition of the books of the Bible in his sermons.[30] Calvin preached twice on Sundays and each day every other week, preaching in excess of four thousand sermons.[31] This was an average of more than 170 sermons each year.[32] Fifteen hundred of them remain to this day, lucid expositions of the meaning of the biblical text interspersed with powerful applications.[33]

It is clear, then, that we must reject the popular and mistaken conception that the totality of Calvin's theology is to be found in the *Institutes*. Brian Armstrong has also provided another warning for everyone engaged in Calvin scholarship, "We must avoid the assumption and natural practice of trying to understand his theology in terms of topoi or loci." "His theology cannot properly be understood

26. Christine Kooi affirms that Calvin "preached and commented on the Old Testament with a thoroughness unmatched by other magisterial reformers." Kooi, "Who Were the Israelites in the Netherlandish Reformation?," 112.

27. Selderhuis, "Calvin, 1509–2009," 149. Cf., De Greef, *The Writings of John Calvin*, 93–109.

28. Manetsch, "Jeremiah in Geneva," 34.

29. Bouwsma, *John Calvin*, 28.

30. Packer, "John Calvin and Reformed Europe," 209.

31. Armstrong, "Exegetical and Theological Principles in Calvin's Preaching," 191.

32. Bouwsma states, "In reviewing the accomplishments of his lifetime on his deathbed, he mentioned his sermons ahead of his writings." Bouwsma, *John Calvin*, 29.

33. Cottret, *Calvin: A Biography*, 289.

as consisting of discrete topics or theological doctrines, but rather must be seen from the perspective of the practical spiritual themes which run like so many threads of a tapestry through all of the ideas basic to his understanding of the Christian message." The threads of a tapestry that Armstrong sees are "the pervasive themes of relationship/communion with/in God, man's response which consists of a trusting worship, adoration and obedience, and similar 'subjective' and 'applied' emphases which permeate his theology from the first page to the last, not just in one particular, discrete section."[34]

There is another dominant theme that runs like a thread through Calvin's commentaries on the Old Testament and New Testament. I am referring to his teaching on the irrevocable call of the Lord to the Jews as his beloved covenant people. This is a doctrine that Calvin ever assumes and to which he continually refers at appropriate points in his preaching and biblical commentaries. That is the subject of this volume, presented in the context of what other significant Reformed theologians and pastors taught on the same subject from Calvin's time to the present.

Literal Hermeneutic

Muller, as has been indicated, maintains that Calvin "took the work of exegesis as his central task and with incredible single-mindedness preached, lectured, and commented through nearly the entire Bible." Furthermore, "he also provided a precedent for highly literal reading of the Old Testament."[35] Calvin, indeed, vigorously rejected the Alexandrian school of allegorical exegesis.[36]

---

34. Armstrong, "The Nature and Structure of Calvin's Thought according to the *Institutes*," 62. Cf., Beeke, "Calvin on Piety," 128. Cottret speaks along similar lines: for Calvin, faith is "a personal relationship with God." "The relationship with God occupied the central place in the life of Calvin." Cottret, *Calvin: A Biography*, 346–47.

35. Muller, "Biblical Interpretation in the 16th & 17th Centuries," 133. Cf., Pitkin, *Calvin, the Bible, and History*, 7.

36. Blacketer, "Calvin As Commentator on the Mosaic Harmony and Joshua," 35. Robert Letham does point out that there were Alexandrians who "interpreted the Bible in a plain and straightforward way." Letham, *Systematic Theology*, 256.

It contended that Scripture hides the truth from the proud, while at the same time it reveals its hidden meaning to the believer who seeks the hidden pearls of truth that are found in the spiritual meaning of the text.[37] "Origen, along with many others along with him," he said, "have seized the occasion of torturing Scripture, in every possible manner, away from the true sense. They concluded that the literal sense is too mean and poor, and that, under the outer bark of the letter, there lurk deeper mysteries, which cannot be extracted but by beating out allegories." He added, "And this they had no difficulty in accomplishing; for speculations which appear to be ingenious have always been preferred, and always will be preferred, by the world to solid doctrine."[38]

Calvin moved away from the medieval quadriga, the idea that Scripture has four meanings—the literal; the allegorical cultivating faith; the tropological nurturing virtue; and the anagogical strengthening hope.[39] He asserted that Scripture has only one meaning, which is literal: "Scripture, they say, is fertile, and thus produces a variety of meanings. I acknowledge that Scripture is a most rich and inexhaustible fountain of all wisdom; but I deny that its fertility consists in various meanings which any man, at his pleasure, may assign."[40]

Although Calvin made some use of rabbinic exegesis, he would not have been attracted by the approach of the Jews who engaged with the Kabbalah and its attempt to uncover the hidden meaning of Scripture by using a cipher method of interpretation.[41]

37. Calvin, *Commentary on the Second Epistle of Paul to the Corinthians*, 172.

38. Calvin, *Commentaries on the Epistle of Paul to the Galatians*, 135. Letham comments regarding Origen, "The general consensus is that his methods opened the door to arbitrary and uncontrolled exegesis." Letham, *Systematic Theology*, 250.

39. Steinmetz, "John Calvin As an Interpreter of the Bible," 284–85; Muller, *Post-Reformation Reformed Dogmatics*, vol. 2, 75.

40. Calvin, *Commentaries on the Epistle of Paul to the Galatians*, 135–36.

41. Austin, *The Jews and the Reformation*, 185. Cooper notes that Giovanni Pico della Mirandola was fascinated with Jewish mysticism and kabbalah and that Johannes Reuchlin who wrote the first Hebrew grammar for Christians was also a promoter of kabbalah studies. Cooper, "Christian Hebraism in the Renaissance and Reformation," 188.

Calvin had a much different hermeneutical perspective: "Let us know, then, that the true meaning of Scripture is the natural and obvious meaning, and let us embrace and abide by it resolutely."[42] It is characteristic for Calvin to refer to the "simple and natural" meaning of a biblical text.[43]

The importance of this commitment to a literal hermeneutic will become clear in the following pages.[44] It indeed is the foundation for his recognition that the Jews as an ethnic people have been and continue to be a special nation loved by God.[45] The ensuing discussion presents some of the main lines of thought that run like threads through the tapestry of Calvin's biblical commentary work. The consideration also includes at various points the reflections of major biblical exegetes in the Reformed tradition who either agreed with Calvin or went in a different direction in their interpretation of passages of Scripture. Chapter 1 considers the issue of Abraham and his biological offspring as being chosen and loved by God. Chapter 2 examines the promise of salvation that was offered to them. Chapter 3 contemplates the matter of their personal responsibility, the need for them to put their trust in the Lord and their failure so often to do so. Chapter 4 reflects upon the solemn theme that the natural Jewish branches of the olive tree of grace were broken off, while the wild olive branches of believing Gentiles have been grafted in and have become part of the covenant people of God. It also reviews the incredible prospect presented in Romans 11 and elsewhere in the biblical revelation that the Jews as a nation are still loved by God and will be saved in the time that the Lord has appointed.

42. Calvin, *Commentaries on the Epistle of Paul to the Galatians*, 135–36.

43. De Greef, "Calvin As Commentator on the Psalms," 94.

44. John L. Thompson notes that one of Calvin's "hallmarks as an exegete" was "his avowed commitment to the 'literal' or 'historical' sense of the text." Thompson, "Calvin As a Biblical Interpreter," 63.

45. Pitkin makes the observation that the exegetical work of Calvin "evidences a deep appreciation of the actual history of the Jewish people." This was "an appreciation he shared with the Antiochian exegetes of the early church." Pitkin, *Calvin, the Bible, and History*, 21.

I

Chosen and Loved by God

"God chose in the person of Abraham a particular people whom he dedicated to himself so that from them the Saviour of the world might descend."[1] This was the kind of message that Calvin's congregants heard when their pastor ascended the pulpit to expound passages in the Scripture regarding the Jews or the Israelites, terms which he used synonymously.[2] This followed his understanding of what Paul does in Romans 1:17. "Under the name *Jew*," affirmed Calvin, "he comprehends all the Israelites, all of whom were then, without any difference, called Jews."[3]

Calvin, like Zwingli, had actual contacts with Jews of his time.[4] While Zwingli discussed Old Testament interpretation with a number of friends along with a Jewish doctor named Mosse, the son of Lazarus, we do not know the names of any of the adherents of Judaism with whom Calvin had discussions.[5] Nevertheless, Calvin maintained that he had experienced personal interactions with them.[6] This was the case, even though they had been officially expelled from his native France in 1394. Geneva had done

1. Calvin, *Sermons on Genesis*, 37.

2. Calvin generally preached on Old Testament texts on weekdays and New Testament texts on Sundays. DeVries, "Calvin's Preaching," 111.

3. Calvin, *Commentaries on the Epistle of Paul the Apostle to the Romans*, 101.

4. Calvin, *Commentaries on the Book of the Prophet Daniel*, vol. 1, 185.

5. Kirn, "Ulrich Zwingli, the Jews, and Judaism," 172–73.

6. Robinson, *John Calvin and the Jews*, 20.

the same thing in 1490.[7] Governmental mandates for their ejection, however, did not necessarily mean an absolute removal from a location. Some of the Italian musicians, for example, at the court of Henry VIII (1491–1547), were of Jewish ethnicity, even though the Jews had been thrown out of England in 1290.[8] Even with the expulsions in France, there may well have been as many as 20,000 Jews still living there when Calvin was born.[9] He may also have met Jewish people when he visited the Duchy of Ferrara and when he resided in Strasbourg.[10] It is indisputable that Calvin had significant contact with the Hebraist Immanuel Tremelius who had converted from Judaism to Christianity and visited Calvin in Geneva.[11]

The Blessing of the Nations

Even apart from his interactions with the Jews of his time, Calvin recognized that the Jewish people were at the very center of the biblical revelation.[12] He determined that he would teach the biblical message that emphasized the central role of the Jewish people in the plan of God. "All the nations of the earth," he declared, "will be blessed in Abraham, and not as regards him but as regards the seed which has descended from him, namely, our Lord Jesus Christ."[13] This was the truth that needed to be heard in Geneva and throughout Europe: the Jews were chosen and loved by God, and Jesus has descended from them.[14] "They were separated for a time from the

---

7. Baron, "John Calvin and the Jews," 380.

8. Austin, *The Jews and the Reformation*, 195.

9. Austin, *The Jews and the Reformation*, 24.

10. Detmers, "Calvin, the Jews, and Judaism," 203–4; Austin, *The Jews and the Reformation*, 80–81; Gordon, *Calvin*, 117.

11. Detmers, "Calvin, the Jews, and Judaism," 207–8; Van Ravenswaay, "Calvin and the Jews," 143–44; De Greef, *Of One Tree*, 66–67.

12. Van Genderen and Velema, *Concise Reformed Dogmatics*, 210.

13. Calvin, *Sermons on Genesis*, 71.

14. Calvin, *Sermons on Genesis*, 71.

rest of the nations on the express condition, that the pure knowl-edge of God should flow out from them to the whole world."[15]

Two twentieth-century Church of Scotland theologians spoke in similar terms.[16] Thomas Torrance (1913–2007) drew at-tention to the connection between the Jews and the Incarnation.[17] He stated, "When at last God came into the world he came as a Jew. And to this very day Jesus remains a Jew while still the eter-nal Son of God."[18] Torrance likewise reflected upon the relation-ship between the Jews and the biblical revelation in the Old and New Testaments: "What ultimately stamps the People of Israel as so distinctive is that they are the people chosen from among the human race for the special purpose of being God's instrument in the mediation of divine revelation and reconciliation to all peoples and nations."[19] We must always remember that it is "through the Jewish scriptures of the Old Testament and the Jewish scriptures of the New Testament church, that the gospel comes to us, and that Jesus Christ is set before us face to face as Lord and savior."[20]

The Scottish pastor and theologian David Torrance had the same perspective: "No one can reasonably dispute that the Chris-tian Church owes her spiritual heritage to Judaism." "The Church," as Calvin specifically stated, "owes to the Jews her understanding of God." But there is more to it than a proper understanding of the-ology proper. Gentile believers through the instrumentality of the Jews have been able to apprehend "his covenant of Grace . . . man as created in the image of God and the nature of God's salvation in Christ, the Scriptures of both the Old and New Testament and

---

15. Calvin, *Commentary on the Gospel according to John*, vol. 1, 160.

16. "Torrance and Taylor, *Israel, God's Servant*, 7.

17. George Hunsinger taught theology at Princeton Theological Seminary for many years. Thomas Torrance in his view was "the greatest Reformed theo-logian since Karl Barth." Hunsinger, "Thomas F. Torrance," 11. Cf., McGrath, *Thomas F. Torrance*, xi.

18. Torrance, *Incarnation*, 43.

19. Torrance, "The Divine Vocation and Destiny of Israel in World His-tory," 88.

20. Torrance, *Incarnation*, 43–44.

the glorious hope of things yet to come under the Hand of God."[21] "God chose the Jews to be the bearers of divine revelation to the world: Abraham, Isaac, Jacob, Joseph, Moses, Samuel, David, Isaiah, Jeremiah, Mary, Jesus, Peter, James, John and Paul." Indeed, "most of the New Testament was written by Jews."[22]

Douglas Kelly reflects similar perspectives as the Torrance brothers on the divine election of the Jews for the purpose of bringing salvific blessing to the entire world.[23] Kelly states, "The entire Old Testament is centered in the history of Israel; Jacob and his descendants are elected to be the bearers of God's blessings to the entire world."[24] What was the basis of the election of Israel to be the people of God? Kelly writes, "Israel was loved and chosen, not for her greatness or wonderful character, but because God set His love upon her." "God as sovereign exercises His mighty love in accordance with His own will, not in accordance with the loveliness of its object."[25] The selection of Israel had in view, as the covenant with Abraham had promised, the blessing of the nations: "There is a major shift of emphasis after the Incarnation, in that non-Jews are now massively brought into the elect covenant community." "Gentiles now become the people of God; sons and daughters of Abraham."[26]

Jerusalem and the Holy Temple

Jerusalem itself had a salvific purpose in the plan of God. Calvin acknowledged that divine providence included all things: "Other cities were founded and built by the guidance and power of God, merely for the sake of civil government." The city of God, though, was different. "Jerusalem was his peculiar sanctuary, and his royal

21. Torrance, "Israel Today, in the Light of God's Word," 105.

22. Torrance and Taylor, *Israel, God's Servant*, 126.

23. Douglas Kelly, Professor of Systematic Theology Emeritus at Reformed Theological Seminary in Charlotte, North Carolina, did his doctoral studies under Thomas Torrance at the University of Edinburgh.

24. Kelly, *Systematic Theology*, vol. 1, 22.

25. Kelly, *Systematic Theology*, vol. 3, 236.

26. Kelly, *Systematic Theology*, vol. 3, 237.

seat."[27] The Lord had an exalted purpose for Jerusalem. It was intended "to have been a faithful guardian of the word of God, a
teacher of heavenly wisdom, the light of the world, the fountain
of sound doctrine, the seat of divine worship, a pattern of faith
and obedience."[28]

In a very real sense, Jerusalem was for a period of time a
unique city: "The pure religion, and the true worship of God, and
the doctrine of godliness, were at that time to be found nowhere
but in Jerusalem." Calvin contemplated the reason why Jerusalem
was chosen by God and "so highly distinguished." "The end of such
a choice," he maintained, "was that there might be some fixed place
in which the true religion should be preserved, and the unity of
the faith maintained, until the advent of Christ, and from which it
might afterwards flow into all the regions of the earth."[29]

Calvin declared in no uncertain terms that God desired in the
days of the Old Testament to have a church that was Jewish, a vast
multitude in its extent.[30] "God wanted to choose Abraham's line
according to the flesh so that it might be his church." "Even though
all people belonged to him, he still wanted to be the Lord in Israel."
"He did not act that way toward all nations and had not manifested
to them his ordinances." "He was in truth the God of the Jews, that
is, the God of the people of Israel."[31] The presence of the temple
in Jerusalem underscored this fact. It reflected the desire of the
Lord to live in the midst of his people: "The temple was a token of
the presence of God."[32] The dwelling of God in the temple did not
mean "that his essence was enclosed in that place." Rather, it was

---

27. Calvin, *Commentary on the Book of Psalms*, vol. 3, 397.

28. Calvin, *Commentary on a Harmony of the Evangelists*, vol. 3, 105.

29. Calvin, *Commentary on the Book of Psalms*, vol. 3, 398.

30. De Greef reflects upon Calvin using the word *church* to designate Israel
as the people of God: "One might get the impression that Calvin has lost sight
of Israel's special position as the people of God. But that is not the case. Calvin
is fully cognizant of the fact that Israel occupies a special place among the
nations." De Greef, "Calvin As Commentator on the Psalms," 95.

31. Calvin, *Sermons on Genesis*, 546.

32. Calvin, *Commentary on the Book of Psalms*, vol. 3, 165.

for the purpose that "his people" might experience "that there he was near at hand, and present with them by his power and grace."[33]

The tabernacle, which preceded the temple, had the same purpose. "We find it difficult to realize," said Calvin, "that God is near us, for we always imagine that he is far away." "If we do not see some apparent sign, it seems to us that there is a long distance between God and us, and that we have no way of approaching him." That is "why there had to be a tabernacle, so as to say: 'Here I am; do not fear that I will not watch over you, and that I will not be prepared to help you in time of need.'"[34]

Eventually in the time of Solomon the tabernacle was replaced by the temple which was intended to be "the sacred abode which God had chosen, in which the covenant of eternal salvation should dwell—the sanctuary from which salvation would go forth to the whole world."[35] In addition, "God intended it to be a pledge to show that Christ was to come."[36]

The Seed of Abraham

The number of the children of Abraham would be beyond human calculation. Calvin noted that "God compares Abraham's line with the stars of heaven." The point was that "Abraham's lineage would be so great that it could not be counted."[37] In fact, "it would be easier to count the sand of the sea than the number of his descendants."[38] This divine promise began to find fulfillment at the time of the exodus. "We see what a great multitude of people came out of Egypt," Calvin marveled. "It grew in a short time in an incredible way." "God had to work above the ordinary course of

---

33. Calvin, *Commentary on the Book of Psalms*, vol. 3, 163.

34. Calvin, *Sermons on 2 Samuel*, 309.

35. Calvin, *Commentary on a Harmony of the Evangelists*, vol. 2, 453.

36. Calvin, *Commentary on the Book of Psalms*, vol. 3, 279.

37. Calvin, *Sermons on Genesis*, 208.

38. Calvin, *Sermons on Genesis*, 463.

nature."[39] "The seed of Abraham is compared to the dust, because of its immense multitude."[40]

A central biblical passage in Calvin's discussion at this point is Genesis 17:7: "And I will establish My covenant between Me and you and your descendants after you in their generations, for an everlasting covenant, to be God to you and to your descendants after you." Calvin firmly rejected the position that the descendants of Abraham in this text are only believers among the Jews and the Gentiles. He declared, "They are deceived who think that his elect alone are here pointed out; and that all the faithful are indiscriminately comprehended from whatever people, according to the flesh, they are descended." "For on the contrary," insisted Calvin, "the Scripture declares that the race of Abraham, by lineal descent, had been previously accepted by God." Indeed, "nothing is more certain, than that God made his covenant with those sons of Abraham who were naturally to be born of him."[41]

The statement "I will be a God to thee and to thy seed after thee" had enormous significance. "As soon as it was said," the "Church was separated from other nations." "Then the people of Israel was received, as the flock of God, into their own fold: the other nations wandered, like wild beasts, through mountains, woods, and deserts."[42] "On account of the promise the Lord took peculiar care of that people, as Paul also declares that 'to them belonged the testament, the promise, and the giving of the Law."[43]

Chosen by Grace Alone

Calvin's teaching regarding the Jews had this as its starting point: "Abraham did not naturally possess this privilege of being chosen by God along with his lineage, but it is wholly because God

39. Calvin, *Sermons on Genesis*, 208.

40. Calvin, *Commentaries on the Book of Genesis*, vol. 1, 376.

41. Calvin, *Commentaries on the Book of Genesis*, vol. 1, 447–48.

42. Calvin, *Commentaries on the Book of Genesis*, vol. 1, 448.

43. Calvin, *Commentary on the Book of the Prophet Isaiah*, vol. 3, 255.

ordered it that way."[44] The choice of Abraham and his descendants underscored divine grace and mercy for a man who was lost in sin. "This calling of Abraham," wrote Calvin, "is a signal instance of the gratuitous mercy of God." "He was plunged in the filth of idolatry; and now God freely stretches forth his hand to bring back the wanderer."[45] "Their fathers," including Abraham, "had dwelt in Chaldea, worshipping idols in common with others, and differing in nothing from the great body of their countrymen."[46] A sovereign divine intervention was what made the difference: "Abraham did not emerge from profound ignorance and the abyss of error by his own virtue, but was drawn out by the hand of God."[47] The status given to Abraham was utterly remarkable. It would have been a "high and honourable" title for him to be regarded as a servant of God, but there was much more given to him. Commenting on Isaiah 41:8, Calvin said, "It was an extraordinary honour which the Lord bestowed on Abraham, when he called him his *friend*."[48]

The man who had worshipped false gods became the friend of God. Abraham did not deserve such grace. His descendants were likewise not worthy in themselves. Calvin contended that they were the recipients of the "undeserved favour" of God. "They did not differ from others so as to excel them in any respect."[49] "The Jews excelled the Gentiles, not of their own nature, not by any right of their own, not by any merits of works, but by a free privilege, because God had adopted them in the person of Abraham."[50] He reiterated, "The children of Israel did not differ from others in any excellency attaching to themselves." Calvin insisted that the divine choice was due to the election of grace: "If it be asked why God preferred one people to others, this pre-eminence will

44. Calvin, *Sermons on Genesis,* 547.

45. Calvin, *Commentaries on the Book of Genesis,* vol. 1, 343.

46. Calvin, *Commentaries on the Book of Joshua,* 272.

47. Calvin, *Commentaries on the Book of Joshua,* 273.

48. Calvin, *Commentary on the Book of the Prophet Isaiah,* vol. 3, 255.

49. Calvin, *Commentary on the Book of the Prophet Isaiah,* vol. 3, 255.

50. Calvin, *Commentary upon the Acts of the Apostles,* vol. 1, 305.

certainly lead us to gratuitous election as to its source."[51] "It so pleased God, who has a right to select this or that person according to his pleasure."[52] Israel "owed the distinction" of their election "not to any excellency of their own, but to the free mercy of God the Father which had been extended to them."[53]

The fact of the matter, as Thomas Torrance put it, is that the Jews were a glaring antithesis of moral excellence: "God selected one race from among all the races of mankind, one of the smallest, and, as Moses said, most beggarly and contemptible of all races, in order to make that race the very instrument of his redemptive purpose to reveal himself to every people and to save all humanity." It is indisputable that "God chose and fashioned the people of Israel." At the same time, it must not be forgotten that "they were the most stubborn and stiff-necked people under the sun."[54]

The covenant with Abraham and his offspring was initiated by the Lord and underscored divine grace. Calvin stressed this idea.[55] This perspective had implications in the way that the covenant came to be described in Reformed theology. David Torrance explained it this way: "God made a covenant of grace with Israel. This covenant made with Abraham was often reaffirmed to patriarchs, prophets and kings." Torrance then referred to some of the constituents parts of the Abraham covenant: "Through it God promised to be their God." "He promised to preserve them and bless them and through them to preserve and bless the world."[56] Torrance also warned against failing to appreciate the full scope of what God had promised Israel. "The Land," he insisted, "belongs to the content of that promise." He then cited the promise given to Abraham in Genesis 13:14–15: "Now lift up your eyes and look

---

51. Calvin, *Commentary on the Book of Psalms*, vol. 5, 302–3.

52. Calvin, *Commentary on the Book of the Prophet Isaiah*, vol. 5, 255.

53. Calvin, *Commentary on the Book of Psalms*, vol. 5, 172.

54. Torrance, *Incarnation*, 41.

55. James Boice commented, "Nothing in their ancestry could possible commend Israel to God. Salvation is always of grace." Boice, *Foundations of the Christian Faith*, 12, 258.

56. Torrance, "The Witness of the Jews to God," 2.

from the place where you are, northward and southward and east-
ward and westward; for all the land which you see I will give to you
and to your descendants for ever."[57]

Redemption for Holiness

The mercy of God, said Calvin, was extended to Israel even when
they had morally fallen in Egypt and when suffering came upon
them which would have destroyed them as a people. He wrote,
"They corrupted themselves in Egypt." "Although God remained
firm in his covenant, yet if we consider the character of the Jews,
they had entirely cut themselves off by their faithlessness." "They
did not differ from the profane Gentiles." "Since they had acted so
perfidiously, they could no longer boast themselves to be Abraham's
children."[58] Referring to Abraham, Calvin noted, "The holy Patriarch, on whom the divine blessing had been specially bestowed,
was unable to curb his posterity, and prevent them from abandon-
ing the true God, and prostituting themselves to superstition."[59]

God found the Jews in a "most miserable state." Calvin reflected on the degree of the afflictions that came upon them, "We
know that scarcely any nation was ever so cruelly and disgrace-
fully oppressed." "No species of disgrace was omitted, and their
life was worse than a hundred deaths."[60] "The Egyptians devised
everything against them, and conspired by all means for their
destruction."[61] The Lord, though, was "compassionate" towards his
people.[62] There was a powerful divine intervention. "God stretched
forth his hand not only for the people's defence, but to carry them
forth against the tyranny of Pharaoh and of all Egypt."[63] Calvin
commented on Ezekiel 16:8 and the statement that God entered

57. Torrance, "Israel Today, in the Light of God's Word," 106.

58. Calvin, *Commentaries on the Prophet Ezekiel*, vol. 2, 95–96.

59. Calvin, *Commentaries on the Book of Joshua*, 273.

60. Calvin, *Commentaries on the Book of Joshua*, 97.

61. Calvin, *Commentaries on the Book of Joshua*, 102.

62. Calvin, *Commentaries on the Book of Joshua*, 99.

63. Calvin, *Commentaries on the Book of Joshua*, 102.

into a covenant with Israel so that they became his bride. At the time of their redemption from Egypt, God joined himself in a special relationship to Israel: "He now compares that union to a marriage. Hence if God would bind his people to himself by marriage, so also he would pledge himself to conjugal fidelity."[64]

The Jews, Calvin maintained, had been chosen by God for the purpose of holiness. "The Lord had sanctified Abraham for himself for this end, that his seed might also be holy." "He thus conferred holiness not only on his person but also on his whole race."[65] "The Jews," affirmed Calvin, "had been chosen from the rest of the world. And their holiness was, that God had deigned to take them as his people, having rejected others, while yet there was by nature no difference between them."[66]

"Abraham's children according to the flesh were separated from the rest of the world."[67] The fact that they had been set apart from the nations was symbolized by the ceremonies imposed upon them by God. "Circumcision, sacrifices, washings, and abstaining from certain kinds of food" were "symbols of sanctification, reminding the Jews that their lot was different from that of other nations."[68] The reality of their "gratuitous adoption of God" was to have moral implications.[69] Calvin observed, "For as the people of Israel were on every side surrounded by heathens, from whom they might have easily adopted the worst examples and innumerable corruptions, the Lord frequently recalled them to himself, as though he had said, 'Ye have to do with me, ye are mine; then abstain from the pollutions of the Gentiles.'"[70]

64. Calvin, *Commentaries on the Book of Joshua*, 103.

65. Calvin, *Commentaries on the Epistle of Paul the Apostle to the Romans*, 426.

66. Calvin, *Commentaries on the Prophet Habakkuk*, 41.

67. Calvin, *Sermons on Genesis*, 548.

68. Calvin, *Commentaries on the Epistle of Paul to the Ephesians*, 237.

69. Calvin, *Commentaries on the Prophet Habakkuk*, 41.

70. Calvin, *Commentaries on the First Epistle of Peter*, 47.

Everlasting Love

Calvin heavily stressed that the divine choice of the Jews flowed out of the special love of God for them. They were not worthy of his paternal love, but it was nevertheless extended to the patriarchs and their offspring in the exodus from Egypt: "God made a gratuitous covenant which flows from the fountain of his pity." "The covenant," he insisted, "flows from God's mercy; it does not spring from either the worthiness or the merits of men."[71] The love of God even continues into the present, said Calvin. It is an ongoing and enduring reality. This was not to deny that there is a universal love, a divine benevolence and beneficence for all. "It is indeed certain," insisted Calvin, "that God's care is extended to the whole human race, yea, even to oxen and asses, and to the very sparrows." "As to the necessaries of life, he performs the office of a Father towards all men." These truths, though, did not nullify the reality of an electing love in God: "He has known his chosen people, because he has separated them from other nations, that they might be like his own family."[72]

The entire history of Israel reflected the love of God for them. It was manifested in the exodus. "They had been loved in childhood. The proof of this love was, that they had been brought out of Egypt."[73] The lovingkindness of God was demonstrated in that "He had made war against a powerful king, had afflicted a most flourishing nation, and had devastated a land remarkable for its extreme fertility, in order to succor a body of despised slaves."[74] Indeed, "by unusual favor this nation was taken from the midst of another." "This was done on no other account but because God had embraced Abraham, Isaac, and Jacob with His love, and persevered in the same love towards their posterity."[75]

71. Calvin, *Commentaries on the Book of the Prophet Daniel*, 146.

72. Calvin, *Commentaries on the Prophet Amos*, 201.

73. Calvin, *Commentaries on the Prophet Hosea*, 386.

74. Calvin, *Commentaries on the Last Four Books of Moses*, vol. 1, 317.

75. Calvin, *Commentaries on the Last Four Books of Moses*, vol. 1, 353.

The exodus was truly a remarkable display of divine love and mercy. The love of God, however, was manifested in the determination of the Lord as to where the Israelites would live and the exact geography of their habitation. Commenting on the statement of Moses in Deuteronomy 32:8 that the Most High set up boundaries according to the number of the sons of Israel, Calvin affirmed, "In the whole arrangement of the world, the object which God had in view was to provide for His elect people: for, although His bounty extends to all, still He had such regard for His own, that, chiefly on their account, His care also extends to others." The governance of history flowed out of the special love of God for his covenant people: "This small body was so precious to God, that he arranged the whole distribution of the world with a view to their welfare."[76]

The love of God for the Jews, affirmed Calvin, was an instance of "inestimable condescension." In the gratuitous adoption of "Abraham and his race," God "in a manner" passes by "the heavens and the earth with all their beauty and abundance" and sets his heart upon "a few obscure men."[77] In addition, the astounding love of God for Israel is seen in the fact that it endures forever. In his exposition of Romans 11, Calvin recognized that the Jews "were for the present alienated from God." This, however, was not the end of the story: "God was not unmindful of the covenant which he had made with their fathers, and by which he testified that according to his eternal purpose he loved that nation."[78]

Calvin here anticipated a point that would be made in the twentieth century by two major European theologians, the Dutch Reformed theologian Herman Bavinck (1854–1921) and also Karl Barth (1886–1968). The Jews, noted Bavinck, had no inherent virtue: "In the case of Israel, one can never speak of its own righteousness: it had been chosen despite its stubbornness." The choice of Israel demonstrates the absolute sovereignty of God: "It is God who has mercy on whom he will." "He promises unconditionally that he will be their God and they will be his people."

76. Calvin, *Commentaries on the Last Four Books of Moses*, vol. 4, 343.

77. Calvin, *Commentaries on the Last Four Books of Moses*, vol. 1, 357.

78. Calvin, *Commentaries on the Epistle of Paul to the Romans*, 440.

God's covenant with the Jews will endure forever: "If history then shows that Israel continually desecrates, abandons, or nullifies the covenant . . . prophecy proclaims that God on his part will never break that covenant and never abandon his people." Indeed, "it is an eternal covenant that cannot fail because it is anchored in the grace of God."[79]

The Swiss Reformed theologian Karl Barth likewise underscored the ongoing reality of the love of God for the Jews, "It is true of them right up to our own day: 'He that toucheth you toucheth the apple of my eye. (Zech 2:8).'" Barth, however, noted, "But no man can touch the apple of His eye. Therefore the Jews can be despised and hated and oppressed and persecuted and even assimilated, but they cannot really be touched; they cannot be exterminated; they cannot be destroyed." To put it positively, "they are the only people that necessarily continues to exist, with the same certainty as that God is God."[80]

In fact, as Thomas Torrance who studied under Barth at the University of Basel affirmed, "He who despises the Jew will only destroy himself."[81] "Think for a moment," advised Torrance, "of poor wretched Germany." Nothing like the Holocaust had ever happened before: "Never in history was there such an out and out attack upon the Jews, such a determination carried out with scientific ruthlessness to destroy Israel." No one can touch the apple of the eye of God with impunity: "Germany had to fail. The Nazi régime had to crash, because the attack upon the Jew was an attack on the purpose of God."[82]

An Eternal Covenant

The everlasting love of God for the Jews had implications for the duration of his covenant with them. Barth insisted that the covenant

79. Bavinck, *Reformed Dogmatics*, vol. 3, 495.
80. Barth, *Church Dogmatics*, vol. 4, part 3.3, 218–19.
81. Torrance, "Salvation Is of the Jews," 173.
82. Torrance, "Salvation Is of the Jews," 171.

between God and Israel was an "eternal covenant." This was true "even where on the ground and in the sphere of the covenant there are serious, even the most serious crises: movement of disloyalty, disobedience and apostasy." Barth repudiated the idea that "the covenant may be dissolved, that at its climax the judgment which breaks upon Israel means the 'setting aside' of the covenant."[83] Torrance set forth the same idea regarding the rebellion of the Jews and the enduring love of God for them: "Israel proved to be disobedient and rebellious again and again." Nevertheless, "God bound himself for ever in a covenant or partnership of steadfast love" with them. "The faithfulness of God," declared Torrance, "is not robbed of its effect by the faithlessness of his people, for he will not let them go but binds them even more closely to himself through all divine judgment and rejection that they may finally be restored and reaffirmed in the fulness of his love."[84]

Calvin had set forth the same position at the time of the Reformation: "It would be impossible for God wholly to forget his covenant" with the Jews. Calvin based this assertion upon the declaration of the Lord in Jeremiah 31:37 that he would only cast off all the seed of Israel if the heavens above can be measured and the foundations of the earth below explored. "God's covenant with Abraham's children," he said, "could no more fail than the laws of nature." "God brings before us these strange and impossible things, that we may know that he will at length be reconciled to his people after having justly punished them."[85] "God's mercy would be perpetual and immeasurable towards the children of Abraham." The Lord's position was immovable: "Though they have deserved to die eternally a hundred times, I will yet have a regard to my covenant and my mercy."[86]

83. Barth, *Church Dogmatics*, vol. 4, part 1, 23.

84. Torrance, "The Divine Vocation and Destiny of Israel in World History," 89.

85. Calvin, *Commentaries on the Prophet Jeremiah and the Lamentations*, vol. 4, 145.

86. Calvin, *Commentaries on the Prophet Jeremiah and the Lamentations*, vol. 4, 146.

Comfort for Us All

What is the history of the Jews as laid out before us in the Old and New Testaments? Torrance reminded us of their perpetual rebellion: "All through their history they fought against God." "They killed the prophets. They contradicted God to his face, and resisted him, proving themselves unworthy of his love." In the end, they "willfully blinded themselves" and "actually crucified the Messiah, the Son of God." God, nevertheless, has ever "held them in unswerving love."[87] "Whatever the Jew does," wrote Torrance, "even if He strikes God in the face, God will keep His Word of mercy and love."[88]

The history of God's undying love for Israel in the past and in the future has a profound application to us in the present. Torrance addresses all who are "overwhelmed with shame at the enmity and treachery" of our own hearts, "and cannot believe that God should love you still." His exhortation is to remember this: "If God still keeps covenant with the Jews, even though he has done unbelievable despite to His love, *God will not break His Word to you.*" What is the Word of God, and how has it been authenticated? "It is sealed forever in the life, death, and resurrection of Jesus: '*Him that cometh to Me I will in no wise cast out*'!"[89]

87. Torrance, *Incarnation*, 44.
88. Torrance, "Salvation Is of the Jews," 168.
89. Torrance, "Salvation Is of the Jews," 173.

2

The Promise of Salvation

CALVIN RECOGNIZED THAT THE covenant that God made with Abraham had several constituents. Genesis 12:2, 3, and 7 draw attention to several distinct promises. The seed and the divine blessing came first: "I will make you a great nation; I will bless you and make your name great; and you shall be a blessing. I will bless those who bless you, and I will curse him who curses you; and in you all the families of the earth shall be blessed." The promise of the land followed: "To your descendants I will give this land." What Calvin designated as "the principal part of the covenant" appears in Genesis 17:7, the promise to Abraham of "an everlasting covenant, to be God to you and your descendants after you."

The Hope of Eternal Life

Calvin was not unique in stressing the relationship of communion effected by the covenant. Heinrich Bullinger (1504–1575) was a contemporary of Calvin in Zurich and a close friend as well.[1] He took the position that the promises "offered in that covenant are not only material but also spiritual." God, affirmed Bullinger, "wishes to be the God of Abraham and his descendants." "God will be their protector, confederate, and savior."[2] Cotton Mather (1663–1728)

---

1. Balserak, *John Calvin as Sixteenth-Century Prophet*, 34.

2. Bullinger, "A Brief Exposition of the One and Eternal Testament or Covenant of God," 110.

in Puritan New England stressed the same idea. "The more *General Promises* made unto Abraham," he stated, "cannot be confined unto *This Life*, and unto *Meer Temporal Blessings*." God "would *Exceedingly Reward* him, in the Enjoyment of *Himself*. But we know, the *Perfect Enjoyment of GOD*, is Reserved for another World."[3]

Calvin stood in continuity with these perspectives. Genesis 17:7 indicates, he affirmed, that "this was a spiritual covenant, not confirmed in reference to the present life only; but one from which Abraham might conceive the hope of eternal life."[4] "This promise brings with it the eternal salvation of souls."[5] Calvin was even willing to refer to "the covenant of salvation which God made with Abram."[6] Indeed, "the covenant of salvation was made with Abraham before any temple or ceremonies were, yea, before circumcision was appointed."[7]

More recently, John Frame contended that the election of Israel was unto salvation.[8] He appealed to Romans 9:4–5 where Paul lists the incredible blessings given to Israel including "the adoption, the glory, the covenants, the giving of the law, the worship, and the promises." Frame stated, "These are all blessings of salvation, the blessings of people who have turned from worshiping idols to serve the living and the true God." Although the promise of salvation was offered to Israel in the Abrahamic covenant, "not all individuals in Israel" would be "eternally saved."[9] There was the necessity of faith, the believing appropriation of Christ and the promise of grace and salvation.

Calvin who never tired of stressing the fallen human condition and the sovereign intrusion of divine grace in salvation stated, "This calling of Abraham is a signal instance of the gratuitous

---

3. Mather, *Genesis*, 929–30.

4. Calvin, *Commentaries on the Book of Genesis*, vol. 1, 450.

5. Calvin, *Sermons on Genesis*, 553.

6. Calvin, *Commentaries on the Book of Genesis*, vol. 1, 349.

7. Calvin, *Commentary upon the Acts of the Apostles*, vol. 1, 305.

8. John Frame is Professor of Systematic Theology and Philosophy Emeritus at Reformed Theological Seminary in Orlando, Florida.

9. Frame, *Systematic Theology*, 215.

mercy of God." He then elaborated, "He was plunged in the filth of idolatry; and now God freely stretches forth his hand to bring back the wanderer. He deigns to open his sacred mouth, that he may show to one, deceived by Satan's wiles, the way of salvation."[10] Grace is especially seen in the promise of God following the great test of Abraham—the command to offer his son Isaac as a burnt offering. The oath of the Lord given to Abraham in Genesis 22:18 included the promise of the Messiah: "In your seed all the nations of the earth shall be blessed, because you obeyed my voice." The provision of a Savior was due to the pure, unmerited favor of God.

The Unconditional Abrahamic Covenant

Similar to Bullinger, Calvin drew attention to the one covenant of God.[11] He understood the Mosaic covenant to be "the renewal of the covenant" that he had made with Abraham. When he entered into "a new covenant with his people" at Sinai, he "bound the people to himself by a fixed law, and prescribed a fixed method of worship."[12] The Mosaic covenant was essentially an accessory to the Abrahamic covenant and as such was conditional, bringing blessing for obedience and ultimately exile for disobedience.[13] The covenant with Abraham, though, had an unconditional aspect to it.[14] What did Calvin mean by this? He asserted, "The treachery and rebellion of the nation did not prevent God from sending forth

10. Calvin, *Commentaries on the Book of Genesis*, vol. 1, 343.

11. Pak, *The Reformation of Prophecy*, 157. Cf., Pak, "A Break with Anti-Judaic Exegesis," 20; Balserak, *Establishing the Remnant Church in France*, 165; Pater, "Calvin, the Jews and the Judaic Legacy," 257; Letham, *Systematic Theology*, 445.

12. Calvin, *Commentaries on the Prophet Ezekiel*, vol. 2, 104–5.

13. Calvin, *Commentary on the Book of Psalms*, vol. 5, 155.

14. We shall discuss in chapter 3 that Calvin could affirm that from a certain perspective the covenant was unconditional, while from another viewpoint it was conditional.

his Son, and this was a public proof that he was not influenced by the consideration of their good conduct."[15]

Calvin did not tire of stressing the sense in which "the covenant was not conditional," acknowledging that "God had not withdrawn his favour from the Jews, having chosen them freely of his grace." He affirmed, "Notwithstanding their efforts, as if it had been of set purpose, to destroy the promises, God met their malicious opposition with displays of his marvelous love, made his truth and faithfulness to emerge in a most triumphal manner, and showed that he stood firm to his own purpose, independently of any merit of theirs."[16]

The unilateral determination of God to fulfill the promises given to Abraham, Calvin noted, is reflected in the ritual connected with the formal inauguration of the covenant in Genesis 15.[17] The Lord promised offspring as innumerable as the stars of heaven who would eventually inherit the land from the river of Egypt to the River Euphrates, and there was a solemn ceremony in connection with these promises. Abraham cut three sacrificial animals in two, a three-year-old heifer, a three-year-old female goat, and a three-year-old ram. He placed each half opposite the other along with a turtledove on one side and a young pigeon on the other. Genesis 15:17 then asserts, "And it came to pass, when the sun went down and it was dark, that behold, there appeared a smoking oven and a burning torch that passed between those pieces." Calvin expounded the symbolism by declaring, "When sacrifices were made in ancient times and animals were cut in two, it was a kind of proclamation: 'If I bear false witness and am deceptive, let me be dismembered in this way; let me be punished in such an unnatural way that everyone will learn from my example.'"[18] This

15. Calvin, *Commentary on the Book of Psalms*, vol. 5, 154.

16. Calvin, *Commentary on the Book of Psalms*, vol. 5, 155.

17. John Frame writes, "The Abrahamic covenant is unconditional in the sense that in it God declares that he will certainly accomplish his own purpose, the blessing of the nations through Abraham. But it is conditional in that those who would receive that blessing must trust and obey." Frame, *Systematic Theology*, 71.

18. Calvin, *Sermons on Genesis*, 458.

was an act of remarkable deference on the part of God: "In order to conform to our smallness, he comes down to us, as if he were forgetting what is proper to his majesty." He helps us in the weakness of our faith accommodating himself to us in his revelation.[19] "He is pleased to have pity on us this way and forget and omit nothing needful for us."[20] The Lord by this act of condescension was demonstrating his firm commitment to the fulfillment of his purposes.

Calvin understood that the promises of the covenant with Abraham really amounted to what he called a "grant."[21] This meant that "when God gave the promise, it could not be destroyed by Abraham's sin. Consequently, God overcame everything that stood in the way of the fulfillment of his word."[22] The plan of God, said Calvin, would be effected. "There had to be only one people to descend from Abraham's race to possess that land." "He wanted his grace and his goodness to be enclosed within it until the coming of our Lord Jesus Christ, for the promise of salvation was like a deposit placed in the hands of Abraham and his lineage."[23]

The Abraham covenant was unconditional, a position forcefully stressed by Calvinist theologians in the twentieth century. Lewis Sperry Chafer (1871–1952), an advocate of the Westminster Confession of Faith, stressed the idea that the covenant with Abraham was unilateral, having no conditions.[24] Chafer declared, "The Abrahamic covenant" is "unconditional in every part of it, being that alone which Jehovah declares He will do for and through Abraham. Being unconditional, it cannot be broken by man."[25] David Torrance similarly stated, "God took the initiative in making

19. Blacketer, "Calvin As Commentator on the Mosaic Harmony and Joshua," 45; Schreiner, "Calvin As an Interpreter of Job," 56.

20. Calvin, *Sermons on Genesis*, 459.

21. Calvin, *Commentaries on the Book of Genesis*, vol. 1, 450.

22. Calvin, *Sermons on Genesis*, 527.

23. Calvin, *Sermons on Genesis*, 204.

24. Spencer, "Reformed Theology, Covenant Theology, and Dispensationalism," 248. John Hannah refers to Chafer's attachment to the Calvinistic theological tradition. Hannah, *An Uncommon Union*, 71, 126, 128, 141, 150, 174, 296.

25. Chafer, *Systematic Theology*, vol. 4, 313.

this covenant and therefore its continuance depends entirely on God. Its continuance does not depend on man." In fact, "Israel by her continual presence today testifies that God is faithful. He does keep his covenant of grace with Israel" despite their "rebellion against him." God "never will break his covenant with Israel. He remains patient and merciful. His purposes of love and redemption remain."[26]

The Promise of the Land

God did more than reveal a bare promise of salvation. Calvin wanted his congregants to know that God gave the land of Canaan as a type of heaven, a pledge of eternal life, a seal of salvation to all who believe. "God informs us he will be the Father of Abraham and his seed," proclaimed Calvin. "He will be the Saviour of those who are allied with him by faith." "True, it is added that he will give to both Abraham and his lineage the land as an inheritance, but that is only a seal to confirm the gift."[27]

The goodness of the Lord for Israel was demonstrated in the actual physical land which they came to possess as an inheritance.[28] Calvin stressed the activity of God when it came to Israel taking ownership of the promised land: "Not only did he bring Abraham out of Chaldea, but he rescued all his people from the bondage of Egypt" and "put them in possession of the land of Canaan."[29] The Lord himself, declared Moses in Deuteronomy 8, was bringing Israel into a good land, a land of brooks, fountains, and springs, indeed a land of incredible bounty. Calvin affirmed, "Its abundance was increased in a new and unwonted manner by the arrival of the people, that God might shew that He had blessed that country above all others for the liberal supply of His children." He made the observation: "As long, therefore, as that land was

---

26. Torrance, "The Witness of the Jews to God," 2.
27. Calvin, *Sermons on Genesis,* 554.
28. Horton, "Covenant Theology," 44.
29. Calvin, *Commentary on the Book of the Prophet Isaiah,* vol. 3, 251.

granted as the inheritance of the race of Abraham, it was remarkable for that fertility which God had promised by Moses."[30]

A Type of the Heavenly Country

The gift of the land was wonderful, but there was something that Israel needed to keep before them in their thinking. The message of the Lord to his people, insisted Calvin, was this: "It is true that you will enjoy the land, but remember that I am calling you to a higher purpose, to worshiping me, to trusting in me, in the knowledge that when you are in my safe keeping, you cannot perish."[31] God did promise the land of Canaan as an inheritance, but "it was not to be the final goal of their hopes, but was to exercise and confirm them, as they contemplated it, in hope of their true inheritance, an inheritance not yet manifested to them." "The promise of the land" was a "symbol" of God's "benevolence" and "a type of the heavenly inheritance."[32] The patriarchs, Calvin maintained, understood that this was the case: "The holy fathers aspired to a celestial country."[33] "Abraham did not consider that land to be the principal gift which his successors were to possess."[34] The same thing was true of his grandson. "Since Jacob confessed himself a pilgrim in the land, which had been promised to him as a perpetual inheritance, it is quite evident that his mind was by no means fixed on this world, but that he raised it up above the heavens."[35]

Richard Gamble picks up on Calvin's perspective regarding the spiritual significance of the land promise.[36] Gamble refers to "the depth and breadth of Abraham's faith" which could "see heaven's door wide open." We, too, as believers in Christ "are attracted

30. Calvin, *Commentaries on the Last Four Books of Moses*, vol. 1, 394.

31. Calvin, *Sermons on Genesis*, 555.

32. Calvin, *Institutes of the Christian Religion*, vol. 1, 451.

33. Calvin, *Commentaries on the Epistle of Paul to the Hebrews*, 285.

34. Calvin, *Sermons on Genesis*, 464.

35. Calvin, *Commentaries on the Epistle of Paul to the Hebrews*, 284.

36. Richard Gamble is Professor of Systematic Theology at Reformed Presbyterian Theological Seminary in Pittsburgh, Pennsylvania.

to heaven because it is real to us." In fact, "although we are pilgrims on this earth, we are not separated from the city of God. The land of promise is in clear view." There is significant continuity between Abraham and us. "Abraham breathed the air of Canaan and was refreshed. We too are given breaths of its sweetness, tastes of the power of the world to come."

Gamble then draws out practical applications: "Our hope for that glorious city can make the future a present reality." In a real sense, "hope can destroy time and seize heaven." The biblical teaching, affirms Gamble, provides a proper perspective on our temporary lives in this world: "We remember that the heavenly Jerusalem is right now undergoing a transformation. The people of God are being gathered into the city each day, and they are arriving from the four corners of the earth." The length of our pilgrimage in this world is determined by God: "Knowing that heaven, the heavenly Jerusalem, is being built following God's perfect timetable, we are not impatient that it is not yet finished for us!" There is much consolation for us as we meditate upon "the golden city," the heavenly Jerusalem. We need to remember that "we will witness and live in this crowning product of the work of God for his church, his bride." What is our great expectation? "We want our knowledge of, and attraction for, that sweeter city to be our greatest comfort as we travel—like Abraham."[37]

A Sign of the World to Come

The promise that Abraham's descendants would inherit the land of Canaan had a fullness of meaning, pointing not only to heaven but also to the eschaton, the world to come. Two nineteenth-century Old Testament scholars, Carl Friedrich Keil (1807–1888) and Franz Delitzsch (1813–1890), affirmed that the promise in Genesis 13:14–15 that the land to the north, south, east, and west would be given to Abraham and his descendants forever demanded an eschatological fulfillment: "Through Christ the promise has been

37. Gamble, *The Whole Counsel of God*, vol. 1, 324–25.

exalted from its temporal form to its true essence; through Him the whole earth becomes Canaan."[38]

Calvin took a similar position. He stated, "Under the type of the land of Canaan, not only the hope of a heavenly life was exhibited to Abraham." Romans 4:13 and its reference to the promise that Abraham would be the heir of the world "rightly teaches us," wrote Calvin, that "the dominion of the world was promised to him." In fact, the same thing is true for "the godly" at the present time: "They enjoy through his mercy and good-will his earthly benefits" as "pledges and earnest of eternal life," "acknowledging heaven, and the earth, and the sea, as their own possessions" until "they enter on the full possession of their inheritance." "Both heaven and earth shall be renewed for this end."[39]

The return of Christ in the thinking of Calvin would not issue forth in a millennial kingdom with a limited duration of time.[40] The Second Coming would bring the eternal state.[41] "Let us not hesitate to await the Lord's coming," he said, "with groaning and sighs, as the happiest thing of all." Concerning Jesus Christ, he stated, "He will come to us as Redeemer, and rescuing us from this boundless abyss of all evils and miseries, he will lead us into that blessed inheritance of his life and glory." "The Lord will receive his faithful people into the peace of his Kingdom, 'will wipe away every tear from their eyes', will clothe them with a robe of glory . . . and rejoicing, will feed them with the unspeakable sweetness of his delights, will elevate them to his sublime fellowship—in fine, will deign to make them sharers in his happiness."[42]

---

38. Keil and Delitzsch, *The Pentateuch*, 200.

39. Calvin, *Commentaries on the Epistle of Paul to the Romans*, 169.

40. Jonathan Edwards, conversely, believed that the millennium was a future event and would last one thousand years. Jue, "A Millennial Genealogy," 400.

41. Holwerda, "Eschatology and History," 127.

42. Calvin, *Institutes of the Christian Religion*, vol. 1, 718.

The Duration of the Land Promise

In continuity with his perspective regarding the ultimate eschatological fulfillment of the land promise, Calvin maintained that the word *forever*, in connection with the possession of the land of Canaan by the descendants of Abraham, did not have the idea of perpetuity. How then did he understand Genesis 13:15: "All the land which you see I give to you and your descendants forever"? He noted that the word *olam* "is taken in various senses in Scripture" and that it "comprises in this place" the "whole period of the law." The promise referred, he insisted, to "that period which was brought to a close by the advent of Christ."[43]

Calvin essentially maintained that history has moved to a new dispensation: "This 'forever' is to refer to the coming of our Lord Jesus Christ because he fulfilled all the figures of the law and the world was at that time renewed, in a manner of speaking."[44] Calvin appealed to the status of the Jews in confirmation of his position. "When it is said that God will give the land to Abraham's seed forever," he declared, "it does not mean that it was actually accomplished." "The Jews are vagabonds today and instead of flourishing and prospering in the land of Canaan, they are, so to speak, rejected by everybody."[45] "Today," said Calvin, "no land is set apart for God's children."[46]

Calvin along with Zwingli did not believe that the land was intended to be held by the Jews as a permanent possession. Neither of them accepted any idea of a future return of the Jews to the land of Israel.[47] The two reformers at this point took a different view than significant church fathers.[48] Justin Martyr in the second century answered in the affirmative to the question raised by Trypho,

43. Calvin, *Commentaries on the Book of Genesis*, vol. 1, 375.

44. Calvin, *Sermons on Genesis*, 211.

45. Calvin, *Sermons on Genesis*, 210.

46. Calvin, *Sermons on Genesis*, 464.

47. Kirn, "Ulrich Zwingli, the Jews, and Judaism," 193–94.

48. Calvin and Zwingli would also have dissented from the views of John Wycliffe and Jan Hus in their position that the Jews would return to the land of Israel. Hill, "Till the Conversion of the Jews," 14.

"Do you really admit that this place, Jerusalem, shall be rebuilt; and do you expect your people to be gathered together, and made joyful with Christ and the patriarchs, and the prophets, both the men of our nation, and other proselytes who joined them before your Christ came?" The answer given by Justin was unambiguous: "I and others, who are right-minded Christians on all points, are assured that there will be a resurrection of the dead, and a thousand years in Jerusalem, which will then be built, adorned, and enlarged."[49]

Irenaeus, a contemporary of Justin, made similar statements regarding an earthly one-thousand-year kingdom of Christ. It would be a time, he said, when the prophecy of Ezekiel 28:25–26 would find fulfillment: "These things saith the LORD, I will gather Israel from all nations whither they have been driven, and I shall be sanctified in them in the sight of the sons of the nations: and they shall dwell in their own land, which I gave to my servant Jacob. And they shall dwell in it in peace; and they shall build houses, and plant vineyards, and dwell in hope, when I shall cause judgment to fall among all who have dishonoured them, among those who encircle them round about; and they shall know that I am the LORD their God, and the God of their fathers."[50]

John Frame contends that the perspectives of the early church fathers carry a lot of weight. "The evidence from the church fathers," he argues, "one or two generations removed from the apostles, is impressive." The "case to be made for premillennialism" likewise rests, according to Frame, on "some Bible passages" that "describe a reign of God on the earth that doesn't seem to fit either the present age or the eternal state." In Isaiah 65:18–20, for example, "God reigns visibly on earth, and yet there is continuing sin and rebellion." Here we have "a prophecy of the last days, in which God reigns on earth." Yet, at the same time, "God has not finally done away with sin and death."[51] Advocates of premillennialism within the Reformed community would insist that such

---

49. Justin Martyr, "Dialogue with Trypho, a Jew," 239.

50. Irenaeus, "Against Heresies," 563.

51. Frame, *Systematic Theology*, 1091–92.

passages necessitate a future millennium preceding the eternal state as presented in Revelation 21 and 22.[52]

Calvin did not embrace the prospect of a future restoration of the Jews to their ancient homeland. He differed from Tertullian in the third century who commented on the fact that "the very land of paternal promise" had been "torn" from the Jews, but further stated that "it will be fitting for the Christian to rejoice, and not to grieve, at the restoration of Israel."[53] Calvin along with Bullinger rejected millennial doctrine. Bullinger declared, "We condemn the Jewish dreams, that before the day of judgment there shall be a golden age in the earth, and that the godly shall possess the kingdoms of the world, their wicked enemies being trodden under foot."[54]

The Restoration of the Kingdom

Calvin denied that there would be a restoration of an earthly Davidic kingdom in the ancient homeland of the Jews. Acts 1:6 presents the record of the apostles asking Jesus whether he would at that time restore the kingdom to Israel. "To restore," Calvin noted, "doth signify to set up again that which was fallen."[55] The Lord responded in Acts 1:7 by saying that it was not for them to know times or seasons which the Father alone had placed under his own authority. Calvin provided significant commentary on this exchange between the apostles and Christ in which he repudiated millennial doctrine: "They dream of an earthly kingdom." "They are also greatly deceived herein, in that they restrain Christ's kingdom unto the carnal Israel, which was to be spread abroad, even unto the uttermost parts of the world."[56] "He meant to drive out

52. Jue states concerning the publication in 1627 of *The Key of Revelation* by Joseph Mede: "Not since the chiliasm of the ante-Nicene church fathers had an individual with orthodox credentials held to a premillennial interpretation of Revelation 20." Jue, "A Millennial Genealogy," 408.

53. Tertullian, "On Modesty," 82.

54. Bullinger, "The Second Helvetic Confession," 853.

55. Calvin, *Commentary upon the Acts of the Apostles*, vol. 1, 44.

56. Calvin, *Commentary upon the Acts of the Apostles*, vol. 1, 43.

of his disciples' minds that fond and false imagination which they had conceived of the terrestrial kingdom."[57] "Those which held opinion, that Christ should reign as a king in this world a thousand years fell into the like folly."[58]

David Torrance had great appreciation for Calvin as a biblical commentator, but he took a radically different approach to the exchange between Jesus and the disciples in Acts 1:6–7. Torrance drew attention to the response of Jesus to the question that the disciples had raised about the timing of the restoration of the kingdom: "Jesus did not reject their question as wrong in itself, he does not deny that there will be a future restoration of the kingdom to Israel, instead he says, 'It is not for you to know times or seasons which the Father has fixed by his own authority.'" Torrance then reasoned, "The restoration of that kingdom however is not possible without a restoration to the Land!"[59] Jesus, in his view, explicitly referred to the restoration of Israel to the land of promise in his declaration regarding the future in Luke 21:24: "Jerusalem will be trodden down by the Gentiles, until the times of the Gentiles are fulfilled." Commented Torrance, "These words clearly imply that a time will come when Jerusalem will not be trodden down by the Gentiles and when Jerusalem will be restored and Israel will again be a people of God in the Promised Land."[60] Furthermore, on the basis of Acts 3:19–21, he maintained that when the Jews repent and "turn to Jesus," their sins would "be blotted out" and "times of refreshing would come" connected with God sending the Christ appointed for them. In other words, we need to recognize that "the returning Christ is also destined for Israel."[61]

Geerhardus Vos (1862–1949) had a different perspective than that advanced by Torrance.[62] He spoke in a disparaging way

57. Calvin, *Commentary upon the Acts of the Apostles*, vol. 1, 47.

58. Calvin, *Commentary upon the Acts of the Apostles*, vol. 1, 48.

59. Torrance, "Israel Today, in the Light of God's Word," 106–7.

60. Torrance, "Israel Today, in the Light of God's Word," 113.

61. Torrance, "Israel Today, in the Light of God's Word," 113.

62. Vos taught at Princeton Theological Seminary in the late nineteenth and early twentieth century.

about chiliasm and the position that Israel dispersed among the nations would be restored to their ancient homeland. The idea that the Lord would appear and "return Israel to the land of Canaan" and that "in a glorified Jerusalem and Canaan, Israel . . . will become a spiritual metropolis for all countries" was a "crass view" according to Vos. He rejected the position that "at the end of the 1,000 years the unbelieving elements of the countries surrounding it will be united, rise up against the Holy Land and besiege the glorified Jerusalem" and "in doing that . . . will be crushed by the Lord, after which the general resurrection, the last judgment, and the end of the world will follow."[63] The position of "an external, national restoration of Israel" and a "national, earthly future for Israel," "restored as a unified people with political, theocratic institutions and external national forms," is a "conception," said Vos, that "is in conflict with Scripture." The reason is this: "With the incarnation and Christ's finished work of satisfaction, Israel's national calling has been terminated." Even "if Israel in its majority had not rejected the Savior," it "would not have been more than the first in the line of Christian peoples, a part of spiritual Israel."[64]

The Issue of Hermeneutics

Calvin and Vos and others within the Reformed tradition articulated where they stood on the issue of Israel and a future restoration to the land. There were other views within the Reformed community, however, that surfaced on the issue of the land of Israel and the restoration of the Davidic kingdom, largely based upon the insistence of applying a consistently literal hermeneutic to biblical prophecy.

Wolfgang Capito already in the sixteenth century taught that there would be a physical restoration of the Jews to the land of Israel before the final coming of the Kingdom of God.[65] Johann

---

63. Vos, *Reformed Dogmatics*, 1139.
64. Vos, *Reformed Dogmatics*, 1140.
65. Pak, *The Reformation of Prophecy*, 100. Cf., De Greef, *Of One Tree*, 54.

Heinrich Alsted (1588–1638) on the Continent and Joseph Mede (1586–1639) in England set forth a premillennial eschatology in the early seventeenth century.[66] In the view of Alsted, the church in her suffering could be comforted by the hope of a future millennium.[67] John Owen (1616–1683) in his commentary on Hebrews declared that there would be a "restoration" of the Jews "unto their own land, with a blessed, flourishing, and happy condition therein."[68] Wilhelmus à Brakel (1635–1711), a major theologian of the Dutch Second Reformation, taught a physical restoration of the Jews to the Holy Land. He asked, "Will the Jewish nation be gathered together again from all the regions of the world and from all the nations of the earth among which they have been dispersed?" He inquired, "Will they come to and dwell in Canaan and all the lands promised to Abraham, and will Jerusalem be rebuilt?" He then answered, "We believe that these events will transpire."[69] He further stated, "Canaan will be extraordinarily fruitful, the inhabitants will be eminently godly, and they will constitute a segment of the glorious state of the church during the thousand years prophesied in Revelation 20."[70]

Calvin recognized that the issue was indeed a matter of whether one would utilize a literal or figurative approach to the prophetic expectation of Old Testament prophecy.[71] In his view the prophets accommodated themselves to the human understanding by frequently employing figures of speech in the proclamations.[72] He used what may be called an analogical reading of Old Testament prophecy.[73] He set forth his basic approach in his commentary on Isaiah 30:25: "When the prophets describe the kingdom of Christ, they commonly draw metaphors from the

---

66. Hesselink, "The Millennium in the Reformed Tradition," 99–100.

67. Jue, "Puritan Millenarianism in Old and New England," 263.

68. Owen, *The Works of John Owen*, vol. 18, 434.

69. Brakel, *The Christian's Reasonable Service*, vol. 4, 530.

70. Brakel, *The Christian's Reasonable Service*, vol. 4, 531.

71. Thompson, "Calvin As a Biblical Interpreter," 68.

72. Pak, *The Reformation of Prophecy*, 292–93.

73. Pak, *The Reformation of Prophecy*, 295.

ordinary life of men; for the true happiness of the children of God cannot be described in any other way than by holding out an image of those things which fall under our bodily senses, and from which men form their ideas of a happy and prosperous condition."[74]

Referring to advocates of chiliasm, he stated, "They applied all such prophecies as did describe the kingdom of Christ figuratively by the similitude of earthly kingdoms unto the commodity of their flesh; whereas, notwithstanding, it was God's purpose to lift up their minds higher."[75] Calvin believed that discussions of the reign of the Lord should focus upon the present: "Christ did then reign when as he subdueth unto himself (all the whole) world by the preaching of the gospel. Whereupon it followeth that he doth reign spiritually, and not after any worldly manner."[76]

A Consistently Literal Approach

Not everyone within the Reformed community has interpreted the prophetic literature of the Old Testament by employing a metaphorical hermeneutic. Although John Charles Ryle (1816–1900) did not refer to Calvin by name, he essentially countered his figurative interpretive approach in a sermon preached in 1868 on behalf of the London Society for promoting Christianity among the Jews.[77] Ryle asked, "What shall we say of the traditional mode of interpreting Old Testament prophecies, in which so many Christians indulge?" He referred to "the system of appropriating all the blessings" promised to Israel in the future "to the Church of Christ." He further specified by talking about "the system of interpreting all prophecies about Christ's first advent literally, and all prophecies about the second advent figuratively."[78] Ryle then answered his own enquiry by asking a question: "What shall we

74. Calvin, *Commentary on the Book of the Prophet Isaiah*, vol. 2, 375.

75. Calvin, *Commentary upon the Acts of the Apostles*, vol. 1, 48.

76. Calvin, *Commentary upon the Acts of the Apostles*, vol. 1, 47.

77. John Charles Ryle, a minister in the Church of England, served as bishop of Liverpool.

78. Ryle, *Are You Ready for the End of Time?*, 110.

say of all these things, but that they are stumbling blocks, great stumbling blocks, in the way of the conversion of the Jews?"[79]

Ryle was a vigorous advocate of a literal approach to biblical interpretation. "Cleave to the literal sense of Bible words," he said, "and beware of that system of allegorizing and spiritualizing."[80] He left this exhortation: "Settle it in your mind, in reading the Psalms and Prophets that Israel means Israel, and Zion Zion, and Jerusalem Jerusalem." "Whatever edification you derive from applying to your own soul the words which God addressed to His ancient people, never lose sight of the primary sense of the text."[81] This meant for Ryle that it needed to be recognized that "the Protestant Reformers were not perfect" and that they were often "much in the wrong" in "the interpretation of Old Testament prophecy." Ryle thus encouraged Christians, "Cast aside the old traditional idea that Jacob, and Israel, and Judah, and Jerusalem, and Zion must always mean the Gentile Church."[82] There is great advantage, he contended, in a consistent literal interpretation of the prophets when it came to Jewish evangelism: "The more we can promote the habit of taking all Scripture in its plain literal sense, the more we are likely to remove prejudices in the minds of honest inquirers in Israel, and to make them hear what we have to say."[83]

Ryle has not been unique within the Reformed exegetical tradition in his commitment to taking the biblical prophecies at face value. More recently, pastor and theologian James Montgomery Boice (1938–2000) insisted upon the necessity of implementing a literal hermeneutic in the handling of Scripture.[84] "Scripture," he said, "is to be interpreted in its natural sense."[85] "There is an obligation to interpret Scripture as literally as possible; that is, to

---

79. Ryle, *Are You Ready for the End of Time?*, 110–11.

80. Ryle, *Are You Ready for the End of Time?*, 100.

81. Ryle, *Are You Ready for the End of Time?*, 101.

82. Ryle, *Are You Ready for the End of Time?*, 144.

83. Ryle, *Are You Ready for the End of Time?*, 111.

84. Boice started the Philadelphia Conference on Reformed Theology.

85. Boice, *Foundations of the Christian Faith*, 96.

take a passage in the literal sense unless it is demonstrably poetic or unless it simply will not bear a literal interpretation."[86]

Boice drew attention to the significant emphasis in the Bible upon the coming of the Messiah into the world.[87] The prophets of the Old Testament announced beforehand both sufferings of Christ and the glories that would follow, but "the greater part of the prophecies concerning the coming of Christ in the Old Testament deal, not with His first advent in which He died as our sin-bearer, but with His second advent in which He is to rule as king." The New Testament reflects back upon his first coming and eagerly anticipates his second coming. In fact, "the Lord's return" is "mentioned 318 times in the 260 chapters of the New Testament."[88] Boice thus advanced a premillennial eschatology: "There must be a literal millennium."[89] Following a great tribulation and the return of Christ, "Satan will be bound for one thousand years. God will establish a perfect government on this earth under Jesus Christ." In harmony with the prophetic expectation, "the earth itself will be transformed, experiencing an increase in fertility."[90] There will be "a golden age" of peace.[91] Specifically, "it will mean the end of the predatory nature of the animal kingdom."[92] "There will be no more war."[93]

A number of interpreters in the Post-Reformation period were committed to a consistent application of a literal hermeneutic. Brakel, for example, insisted that the word *Israel* in the Scripture is

---

86. Boice, *The Last and Future World*, 26.

87. Boice maintained that there are two stages in the Second Coming of Christ: "His return, in part, will be to take His followers to be with Him in heaven. Shortly after that He will appear on earth bodily to set up an earthly kingdom." Boice, *The Last and Future World*, 14.

88. Boice, *The Last and Future World*, 33.

89. Boice, *The Last and Future World*, 27.

90. Boice, *The Last and Future World*, 29.

91. Boice, *The Last and Future World*, 14.

92. Boice, *The Last and Future World*, 29–30.

93. Boice, *The Last and Future World*, 30.

an actual reference to the nation of Israel.[94] He wrote, "God had given Jacob the name of Israel after he had wrestled with the Lord, and his descendants were called by this name." "Throughout the entire New Testament the name Israel is never assigned to believers, that is, the church of the New Testament." "It is always understood," said Brakel, that this refers to the Jewish nation; that is, in distinction to and separation from all other nations."[95]

A Premillennial Eschatology

A strict commitment to a literal hermeneutic among many of the Puritans in the seventeenth century led to a flourishing of premillennialism.[96] Robert Baillie (1599–1662), a Scottish delegate to the Westminster Assembly, complained about the number of chiliasts in attendance.[97] We find the same chiliast outlook in the teaching of the New England Puritan Increase Mather (1639–1723) who saw an ongoing significance to the land of Israel and believed in a restoration of the Davidic kingdom in the future. "The Israelites shall be in their own land again," Mather insisted.[98] Their restoration to the land would be followed by a military invasion from the north: "The Turkish *Ottomanical family*, shall after the *Israelites* are gathered out of the Eastern and Northern parts, and repossessed of the Holy Land, endeavor with great fury to destroy them

94. Vos, conversely, affirmed, "According to the repeated witness of the New Testament, 'Israelite' is synonymous with 'Christian.' The circumcision of the heart makes one a true Jew." Vos, *Reformed Dogmatics*, 1140. I would maintain that the term *Israel* can refer to Jews who are truly saved (regenerate Israel), and it can refer to Israel as an ethnic entity, the Jewish people. We see this in Romans 9:6: "They are not all Israel who are of Israel." The Scripture in addition presents at least two additional meanings. *Israel* can refer to an individual person, namely Jacob. The designation *Israel* can also be used for the organized nation of Israel, a political body.

95. Brakel, *The Christian's Reasonable Service*, vol. 4, 511.

96. Hesselink, "The Millennium in the Reformed Tradition," 100; Austin, *The Jews and the Reformation*, 190.

97. Jue, "Puritan Millenarianism in Old and New England," 265.

98. Mather, *The Mystery of Israel's Salvation*, 36.

(*scil.* At the battel of *Armageddon.*)." The enemies of Israel would fail in this endeavor: "This furious Turk shall come to his end, and then will follow that glorious salvation of *Israel.*"[99]

Mather understood that there were biblical scholars who rejected the idea of a future earthly kingdom: "There are many mistakes about this matter. Some deny that ever the Saints shall have a glorious kingdom upon the earth."[100] Mather, though, saw great significance in the statement in Luke 1:32–33 that Jesus would be given the throne of his father David and that he would reign over the house of Jacob forever in a kingdom that would have no end.[101] He stated, "Surely *the Throne of David* denoteth more than Internal or Ecclesiastical kingdom: Now this Davidical kingdom shall Christ possess after the conversion of the *Jews,* and re-union of all the Tribes."[102] Furthermore, commenting on Acts 1:6–7, Mather stated, "Christ did never absolutely deny his having such *a visible glorious kingdom upon earth,* as that which his Disciples then looked for, only he corrected their errour as to the time of this kingdoms appearing." He insisted, "Christ did not say to them, that there should never be any such restauration of the kingdom to *Israel,* as their thoughts were running upon, only telleth them that the times and seasons were not for them to know, thereby acknowledging that such a kingdom should indeed be as they (for the substance of it) did from the holy Prophets expect."[103]

Mather believed in a premillennial return of Christ to the earth. "Jesus Christ," he maintained, "will be personally present" when "the times of refreshing shall come."[104] "In the glorious restitution of all things, Jesus will come again from heaven." "The

99. Mather, *The Mystery of Israel's Salvation,* 29.

100. Mather, *The Mystery of Israel's Salvation,* 135.

101. Ryle commented, "The words which the angel Gabriel addressed to the Virgin Mary have never yet been fulfilled: 'He shall reign over the house of Jacob for ever; and of His kingdom there shall be no end' (Luke 1:33)." Ryle, *Are You Ready for the End of Time?,* 145.

102. Mather, *The Mystery of Israel's Salvation,* 61.

103. Mather, *The Mystery of Israel's Salvation,* 131–32.

104. Mather, *The Mystery of Israel's Salvation,* 138.

glorious *Sabbatism* which remains for the Saints upon earth will begin at Christ's coming from heaven to judge the world."[105] "The glorious kingdom which Christ with his Saints shall have upon earth, will not be till the great day of judgment," "that blessed thousand years *John* speaketh of."[106] The millennium would be a golden age of peace and prosperity with a miraculous transformation in the order of nature. Mather affirmed, "Then shall such a day as this come upon earth, even a day wherein the Nations shall learn War no more." There will be "that glorious tranquility, which the most high" will "establish on earth."[107] "The time will come when the Land of *Israel* shall be made exceedingly fruitful."[108] Nature itself will undergo a radical change: "Before the fall; the Woolf and the Lamb; the Bullock and the Lion could live quietly by one another, man was not subject to hurt by serpents or venomous creatures, there was not that enmity in any of the creatures to seek the destruction of one another. Even this shall it be again."

Return to the Promised Land

Beginning with Wolfgang Capito, Reformed theologians through the centuries have affirmed their belief that the Bible prophesies a restoration of the Jews to their ancient homeland. The reestablishment of the state of Israel in the twentieth century has been interpreted by significant Reformed thinkers as the fulfillment of prophetic passages such as Amos 10:14–15 arguing that the passage refers to the return of the Jews to the land along with their permanent possession of it.

David Torrance in reflecting upon Genesis 12:3 affirmed concerning the nations of the world: "In loving Israel they have been blessed and in hating and persecuting Israel they have encountered God's displeasure." Citing one example, Torrance stated, "In

---

105. Mather, *The Mystery of Israel's Salvation*, 139.
106. Mather, *The Mystery of Israel's Salvation*, 140.
107. Mather, *The Mystery of Israel's Salvation*, 160.
108. Mather, *The Mystery of Israel's Salvation*, 122.

promoting the Holocaust, Hitler promised the final solution of the Jewish problem, with the extinction of the Jews. Hitler fell and in a short space of time the Jewish people, delivered from the gates of death, became a nation restored to the Promised Land." He then exclaimed, "What a witness to the hand of God!"[109] "In our time, we have seen God gather his people and bring them back from North, South, East and West (from some ninety different countries) and established them again in the Promised Land."[110]

Torrance did not see the Jews and their present return to the land as being a peripheral and inconsequential matter. Regarding recent events as prophetically significant had implications with respect to international politics. Torrance drew attention to Amos 9:15 and the statement of the Lord: "I will plant them upon their land, and they shall never again be plucked up out of the land which I have given them." Said Torrance, "If we interpret this prophecy about the future restoration of Israel in terms of today (and we cannot rightly relate it to any previous period in Israel's history), and if we see in present events the commencement of the fulfillment of this prophecy, then we can say that Israel will never again leave the Promised Land."[111]

Torrance spelled out the implications of this belief in Israel's permanent possession of the land promised to them in the Abrahamic covenant and reiterated in the prophets. "The Bible indicates," he said, "that there will come mounting pressure against Israel and mounting opposition, from all the other nations of the world, as they continue to resist God." These pressures against Israel will be "political, economic and military." They will be "imposed by the nations, in their resistance to God." As we observe ongoing developments in the international political arena, we may note that "the resistance of the nations to God and his way of salvation is increasingly manifest in their opposition to Israel." What outcome can be expected on the basis of the prophetic revelation? Torrance here calls our attention to passages such as Zechariah 12:9 in which

109. Torrance, "The Witness of the Jews to God," 10.

110. Torrance and Taylor, *Israel, God's Servant*, 117.

111. Torrance, "Israel Today, in the Light of God's Word," 107.

the Lord announces that he will destroy all the nations that come against Jerusalem: "God will judge every nation by its attitude to Israel." Nations "that seek to break Israel will themselves be broken and nations that go against Israel will be opposed by God."[112]

The return of the Jews to their ancient homeland should be seen according to Torrance as the fulfillment of the prophetic expectation, but it also has eschatological implications: "The restoration of a remnant to the Promised Land, in itself the fulfillment of prophecy, points forward to the fulfillment of those greater prophecies concerning the new creation, to the renewal of all God's people living on an earth renewed and made perfect."[113] We are living, said Torrance, at a time of great eschatological significance: "It would seem that the present restoration of the land, the causing of the wilderness to blossom like a rose, must be regarded as a foretaste of the coming renewal of heaven and earth."[114] In fact, the formation of the "Jewish state" in 1948 "is an astonishing miracle, an evidence of God's hand at work in history, a clear sign pointing us forward to Jesus' return."[115]

The Imminent Coming of Christ

The return of the Jews to the land promised to them in the Abrahamic covenant indicates for David Torrance that we are on the verge of the Second Coming of Christ: "Israel is a living prophetic message that God is about to do something big and dramatic on this earth. He, the Lord of all history, is calling the nations of the world today to reckon with God." What specifically is God doing? "He is warning them that at the last, which may even be tomorrow, they must give account to him, who is Redeemer, Judge and King."[116]

112. Torrance, "Israel Today, in the Light of God's Word," 111.

113. Torrance, "The Witness of the Jews to God," 11.

114. Torrance, "The Witness of the Jews to God," 11–12.

115. Torrance and Taylor, *Israel, God's Servant*, 115.

116. Torrance, "The Witness of the Jews to God," 12.

Thomas Torrance had similar perspectives as those set forth by his brother David Torrance. He reflected upon what happened in 1948: "The establishment of the new State of Israel, following hard upon the most harrowing ordeal of suffering the Jews have known, is surely the most significant sign given by God in his providential dealings with his covenanted People since the destruction of Jerusalem in A.D. 70."[117] Torrance considered the eschatological significance of the return of the Jews to the land promised to them in the Abrahamic covenant: "The intense actualization" of "God's covenanted communion with the people of Israel within the land of promise, now called Israel, brings home to us in a new way" the "fact that the people and the land are woven invisibly together." But there is more. What has happened in recent history "constitutes God's sign-post in the history of world-events."

What did Torrance mean by this? It is interesting that he called attention to Jerusalem: "In the providence of God Jerusalem, the mother of faith in the living God, is once more the spiritual and physical centre of the people of Israel." He added, "And that is as it should be." In fact, "as the mother of faith in the living God, Jerusalem is the appointed centre for ever by the death and resurrection of Jesus Christ for the one Church of God, Jewish and Christian." The present status of Jerusalem as the capital of Israel also looks to the future. It is "the concrete pledge that Jesus Christ will come again to take up his Kingdom and reign in divine peace over all peoples and nations in a renewal of creation which will far surpass anything that we can conceive in terms of human experience and history hitherto."[118]

Our Redemption Draws Nigh

There are two great signs of the times, contended Thomas Torrance. First, there was a crime beyond imagination, "the extermination

117. Torrance, "The Divine Vocation and Destiny of Israel in World History," 94.

118. Torrance, "The Divine Vocation and Destiny of Israel in World History," 104.

of more than six million Jews."[119] Somewhere between one third
and one half of the world's Jewish population perished in the Holocaust.[120] The second sign is a marvel beyond conception, "the
incredible fact that the Jews are back in Palestine with their own
state, for the first time in ages and ages of history." There has been
nothing comparable in history over the course of two millennia:
"Never since A.D. 34, when Jesus was crucified, and since A.D. 70,
when Jerusalem was destroyed, has God given two such signs in
the world." These two signs have eschatological significance: "Once
again, the Jew stands out in history as God's finger pointing to the
future." What is the Lord saying to us? "Surely this: that God is
about to act in history, about to do a tremendous thing!" Torrance
then appealed to the Gospels in which Jesus said that when we
see the signs of the times, "then get ready." Specifically, "trim your
lamps. Gird up your loins. Watch and pray, for your redemption
draws nigh." There is a message from God "to us in this day of
grace, sent to us by a Jew: *Salvation is at the door!*"[121]

---

119. Torrance, "Salvation Is of the Jews," 172.

120. Torrance and Taylor, *Israel, God's Servant*, 114.

121. Torrance, "Salvation Is of the Jews," 172.

3

The Necessity of Faith

THE COVENANT ESTABLISHED BY God with Abraham extended
to his physical offspring. It was made with the patriarch and with
Isaac and with Jacob and the succeeding generations. Calvin saw
great significance in the reference to generations in Genesis 17:7.
"This succession of generations," he commented, "clearly proves
that the posterity of Abraham were taken into the Church, in such
a manner that sons might be born to them, who should be heirs
of the same grace."[1] "It was not for a day, he would say, or for a
few days, that God has made a covenant with Abraham, nor has
he limited the continuance of his covenant to the life of man, but
he has promised to be the God of his seed even to a thousand
generations."[2] The same message appeared in his preaching: "Our
Lord wanted to show his bounty and continue it in their behalf
from generation to generation and from hand to hand, and he offered himself to the Jews as their Father."[3]

A Unilateral Covenant with Conditions

The same genealogical principle, contended Calvin, appeared in
the time of Moses. Indeed, in his view the Mosaic covenant was
not a different covenant than the covenant that God had made

1. Calvin, *Commentaries on the Book of Genesis*, vol. 1, 450.
2. Calvin, *Commentary on the Book of Psalms*, vol. 4, 178.
3. Calvin, *Sermons on Genesis*, 547.

with Abraham and should be regarded as a renewal of it. The covenant that God made with Abraham was "an eternal, and inviolable covenant," but "it had grown into disregard from the lapse of time." It therefore "became needful that it should be again renewed. To this end, then, it was engraved upon tables of stone, and written in a book, that the marvelous grace, which God had conferred on the race of Abraham, should never sink into oblivion."[4]

Other Reformed thinkers would see more of a distinction between the Abrahamic and Mosaic covenants. The Post-Reformation theologian Herman Witsius (1636–1708), for example, affirmed that the covenant with Abraham was "not to be confounded with" the "Sinaitic covenant." "The Abrahamic covenant," he said, was "a pure covenant of grace and hence were derived the spiritual and saving benefits of the Israelites." Conversely, "the national covenant made with the Israelites at mount Sinai" was more of a bilateral arrangement. "The people promised obedience to God; and God promised the people, that, if they performed that obedience, he would accept and reward it."[5] Michael Horton likewise distinguishes between the Abrahamic covenant asserting that it is a "royal grant" and the Mosaic covenant which is "dependent on Israel's obedience."[6] He observes, "Although Israel inherited the land by a gracious promise that God made to Abraham, the covenant that Israel swears at Mount Sinai is the condition for remaining in the land." "The terms" of the Sinai covenant "are far from the unilateral oath that God made to Abraham in Genesis 15." "Israel" is "to occupy the land as a new Adam under probation."[7] Horton adds, "At Mount Sinai, Moses delivered the covenant to the people, with its commands and sanctions: long life in the land for obedience, and the threat of being cut off, exiled from the land of the

---

4. Calvin, *Commentaries on the Last Four Books of Moses*, vol. 1, 313.

5. Witsius, *The Economy of the Covenants between God and Man*, vol. 2, 336–37.

6. Horton, *The Christian Faith*, 537. Michael S. Horton is the J. Gresham Machen Professor of Systematic Theology and Apologetics at Westminster Seminary California.

7. Horton, *The Christian Faith*, 440.

living, for disobedience." "Israel did not fulfill its commission and was exiled from the temporal and typological garden of God."[8]

Calvin, though, made less of an effort to distinguish between the two covenants—the Abrahamic formally inaugurated with the shedding of blood in Genesis 15:18 and the Mosaic established with sacrificial blood in Exodus 24:8.[9] He firmly stated, "It is certain indeed that the same covenant, of which Abraham had been the minister and keeper, was repeated to his descendants by the instrumentality of Moses."[10] He could affirm that the Abrahamic covenant was unconditional and likewise affirm that it had conditions.[11] In his biblical commentary on Romans 9:4, Calvin maintained that the covenant with Abraham had conditions for both parties: "A covenant is that which is expressed in distinct and accustomed words, and contains a mutual stipulation, as that which was made with Abraham."[12]

Mercy for a Thousand Generations

The Lord in connection with the giving of the Second Commandment announced that he is a God who shows love to a thousand generations of those who love him and keep his commandments. Calvin reflected upon this remarkable statement: "He declares that He will be merciful even to a thousand generations." "He declares that He will be kind, not only to themselves, but to their posterity, even for a thousand generations."[13] This did not mean that everyone who descended from Abraham would find salvation. "Grace

---

8. Horton, *The Christian Faith*, 493.

9. Steinmetz writes, "For Calvin there was one covenant and one people of God in both testaments." Steinmetz, "John Calvin As an Interpreter of the Bible," 286.

10. Calvin, *Commentaries on the Last Four Books of Moses*, vol. 1, 314.

11. Muller states, "Calvin notes how from one perspective the covenant is unconditional and from another, conditional." Muller, *The Unaccommodated Calvin*, 155.

12. Calvin, *Commentaries on the Epistle of Paul to the Romans*, 340.

13. Calvin, *Commentaries on the Last Four Books of Moses*, vol. 2, 111.

is not promised severally to all the posterity of the saints," Calvin cautioned. The history of Israel was well known: "There were many degenerate children of Abraham, to whom it profited nothing that they were called the offspring of the holy patriarch."[14]

The generational love of God does mean, however, that "the goodness of God ever superabounds so that His grace, if it does not shine with full splendor, still appears in bright sparks unto a thousand generations."[15] The bright sparks of grace that Calvin had in mind included such things as "temporal blessings" as well as "the Law, the Prophets, the Temple, and other exercises of religion."[16] This truly is a remarkable divine attribute: "God's liberality is an inexhaustible fountain, which will never cease to flow so long as its progress is not impeded by the ingratitude of men." Calvin understood that human sin might well block the flowing of the fountain of grace, but God wanted the free flow of generational grace. "And hence," he mused, "it will be continued to their posterity, because God manifests the grace and fruit of his adoption even to a thousand generations."[17]

Election among the Chosen People

Genealogical descent from Abraham brought incredible blessing, but by itself did not bring salvation. "All those who descended from that race according to the flesh are not considered true Israelites," declared Calvin. The reality of an Ishmael and an Esau was enough to prove his point.[18] They "were rejected just as if they were strangers; even though they were real offspring of Abraham according to the flesh." "Salvation depends upon God's mercy, which he extends to whom he pleases."[19]

14. Calvin, *Commentaries on the Last Four Books of Moses*, vol. 2, 112.

15. Calvin, *Commentaries on the Last Four Books of Moses*, vol. 2, 113.

16. Calvin, *Commentaries on the Last Four Books of Moses*, vol. 2, 112.

17. Calvin, *Commentary on the Book of Psalms*, vol. 4, 354.

18. Calvin, *Sermons on Genesis*, 548.

19. Calvin, *Institutes of the Christian Religion*, vol. 2, 1336.

There was then a twofold election with respect to Israel, a general election of the nation and a narrow election unto salvation. "That second election" was "confined to a part only."[20] "Some men are by special privilege elected out of the chosen people, in whom the common adoption becomes efficacious and valid."[21] Great privilege came to all, but not saving grace: "There was a difference between the natural children of Abraham, that though all were adopted by circumcision, into a participation of the covenant, yet the grace of God was not effectual in them."[22] "As the blessing of the covenant separates the Israelite nation from all other people, so the election of God makes a distinction between men in that nation."[23]

There had to be an appropriate response to the covenant embrace of God. Calvin took the same position that Bullinger espoused in his exegesis of the divine command given in Genesis 17:1: "Walk before Me, and be blameless." Bullinger said, "The phrase 'to walk' according to Hebrew usage is the same as 'to live.'" "And God adds, 'before me,' which means 'according to my will and pleasure.'" "It is our duty to adhere firmly by faith to the one God."[24] Calvin concurred with Bullinger regarding the absolute necessity of faith. He reflected, for example, upon the warning of John the Baptist addressed to the Pharisees and Sadducees in Matthew 3:9 that they should not trust in mere physical descent for their salvation. He commented, "None are entitled to be regarded as belonging to 'the seed of Abraham,'" but "those who follow his faith, and that without faith the covenant of God has no influence whatever in procuring salvation."[25]

True saving faith entailed yielding oneself to God: "The children of Abraham were separated from other nations; so that, relying upon this privilege, they might unhesitatingly and unreservedly surrender themselves to a father so benignant and

---

20. Calvin, *Commentaries on the Epistle of Paul to the Romans*, 345.

21. Calvin, *Commentaries on the Epistle of Paul to the Romans*, 346.

22. Calvin, *Commentaries on the Epistle of Paul to the Romans*, 348.

23. Calvin, *Commentaries on the Epistle of Paul to the Romans*, 349.

24. McCoy and Baker, *Fountainhead of Federalism*, 111.

25. Calvin, *Commentary on a Harmony of the Evangelists*, vol. 1, 190.

bountiful."[26] Trusting in God and surrendering one's life to him meant responding to the covenant with obedience: "God is merciful only to *those who*, on their part, *keep his covenant*, which the unbelieving make of none effect by their wickedness."[27]

There was always a remnant in Israel who believed, "a hidden seed of the election remained among them."[28] "The Jews," Calvin acknowledged, "had become so perverted that, in the time of our Lord Jesus Christ, there was almost no longer a trace of that covenant." "They were filled to overflowing with vice, and it appeared as if they plotted against God to cast him from themselves." But the apostasy, although widespread, was not universal. "God had preserved some seed. Even though they were few, there still remained a remnant." What was the reason for this? "Because God's election, Paul says, is irrevocable."[29]

The call of God to the children of Abraham, though, went unheeded on the part of many. In fact, "although God adopted all of Jacob's line," Calvin was willing to say that "the majority of them broke away from him."[30] This meant that there was "a twofold class of sons" in Israel—the genuine and the false. "We therefore distinguish," wrote Calvin, "the true from the spurious children, by the respective marks of faith and unbelief." He put it this way: "All without exception, are, in this respect, accounted children; the name of the Church is applicable in common to them all: but in the innermost sanctuary of God, none others are reckoned the sons of God, than they in whom the promise is ratified by faith."[31]

26. Calvin, *Commentary on the Book of Psalms*, vol. 4, 354.

27. Calvin, *Commentary on the Book of Psalms*, vol. 4, 140.

28. Calvin, *Commentaries on the Book of Genesis*, vol. 1, 450.

29. Calvin, *Sermons on Genesis*, 559.

30. Calvin, *Sermons on Genesis*, 311.

31. Calvin, *Commentaries on the Book of Genesis*, vol. 1, 449.

Criminality beyond Imagination

"Their chief crime was unbelief."[32] Calvin here was reflecting upon the Jewish people as they are presented in the biblical revelation. This is a remarkable statement due to the fact that Calvin's writings provide a full spectrum of reflection on the sins of the Jews as presented in Scripture.[33] Medieval theology presented seven capital sins—pride, avarice, envy, anger, lust, gluttony, and sloth—but Calvin bypassed all of these by drawing attention to the root sin, the fundamental problem of unbelief.

There were other issues, though, that Calvin drew attention to when it came to the sins of the children of Abraham. He drew attention to their lack of thankfulness along with their scorning of the privilege of being called by God. He commented on the statement in Luke 19:41 that when Jesus drew near to the city of Jerusalem, he wept over it: "When he saw the people, who had been adopted to the hope of eternal life, perish miserably through their ingratitude and wickedness, we need not wonder if he could not refrain from tears."[34] He added this remark concerning Jerusalem: "There never certainly was a city in the world in which God bestowed such magnificent titles, or such distinguished honour; and yet we see how deeply it was sunk by its ingratitude."[35]

Their absence of gratefulness was accompanied, maintained Calvin, with contempt toward all the advantages bestowed upon them in the covenants and promises. The Jews, he noted, were remarkably benefited by God. "Abraham's lineage was chosen and adopted by God and consequently made a holy and sacred lineage, a priestly kingdom." "Yet little has been gained by those who scorned the great privilege of being called by God."[36] Their behav-

32. Calvin, *Commentaries on the Epistle of Paul to the Romans*, 440.

33. Robert Michael suggests that the Christian Scriptures reflect antisemitism and express "an anti-Jewish invective." We need to remember, however, that Jesus and the apostles were Jews. Michael, "Antisemitism and the Church Fathers," 103.

34. Calvin, *Commentary on a Harmony of the Evangelists*, vol. 2, 453.

35. Calvin, *Commentary on a Harmony of the Evangelists*, vol. 3, 106.

36. Calvin, *Sermons on Genesis*, 551.

ior was totally unreasonable: "That was their great condemnation because they were so wicked and perverse as to reject that incomparable privilege and make themselves unworthy of the heavenly inheritance that was offered to them."[37] This was not a light matter. "No offence," insisted Calvin, "is more heinous in the sight of God, than obstinacy in despising his grace."[38]

Their unbelief, ingratitude, and scorn were linked with the vices of pride and hypocrisy, which reflected the fundamental problem of spiritual blindness.[39] Near the end of his earthly ministry, Jesus expressed his longing and desire in Matthew 23:37 to gather together the children of Abraham to himself as a hen gathers her chicks under her wings. The Jews, though, were not willing to come to him for salvation. Their problem, said Calvin, was their pride: "Since God attempted to draw the Jews to himself by mild and gentle methods, and gained nothing by such kindness, the criminality of such haughty disdain was far more aggravated."[40] There is no hope for those who give way in their lives to such prideful defiance of God: "This is the crowning point of desperate and final depravity, when men obstinately reject the goodness of God, and refuse to come *under his wings*."[41] Their pride in the days of Jesus was nothing new. In his commentary on Jeremiah, Calvin wrote, "The Prophet laboured to lay prostrate their pride and arrogance." Jeremiah, though, ministered in vain. "They laughed at all threatenings, and remained ever secure; though God, as it were, with an armed hand and a drawn sword menaced them with certain destruction, yet nothing moved them."[42]

37. Calvin, *Sermons on Genesis*, 552.

38. Calvin, *Commentary on a Harmony of the Evangelists*, vol. 3, 136.

39. Richard Gamble highlights the prophet Hosea and his indictment of Israel: "There was no faithfulness, kindness, or understanding." "She became proud and forgot God." Gamble, *The Whole Counsel of God*, vol. 1, 595.

40. Calvin, *Commentary on a Harmony of the Evangelists*, vol. 3, 106.

41. Calvin, *Commentary on a Harmony of the Evangelists*, vol. 3, 108.

42. Calvin, *Commentaries on the Prophet Jeremiah and the Lamentations*, vol. 3, 430.

Their hubris led them to manipulate the biblical text. Commenting on Genesis 16:13 and the appearance of the Angel of the LORD to Hagar, Calvin wrote, "Some among the Hebrews say that Hagar was astonished at the sight of the angel; because she thought that God was nowhere *seen* but in the house of Abram." He then stated, "In this way the ambition of the Jews often compels them to trifle; seeing that they apply their whole study to boasting of the glory of their race."[43]

Their pride led them to a vain pursuit. They "sought to be justified by works, and thus laboured for what no man could attain to."[44] "They sought to set up a righteousness of their own."[45] In reality, they were nothing but hypocrites. "That is the way it was with Abraham's lineage," declared Calvin. They had a special status by virtue of God's covenant with them. "God had chosen all of them and borne witness to them that he would be their Father and Saviour." "On the one hand, they are the holy lineage and, on the other, they are wicked and polluted, as Jerusalem was called a holy city and a den of robbers."[46]

Their pride in their self-righteousness linked with hypocrisy was accompanied by their hatred of the gospel. "The Jews," wrote Calvin, "do not merely despise the gospel, but even abhor it."[47] They "raged against the gospel with unbounded fury."[48] Reflecting upon Acts 17:13, Calvin wrote, "The Jews were carried to and fro with such hatred of the gospel as could never be appeased."[49] All of this reflected an inability to perceive spiritual truth: "It was owing to their blindness, that they did not make any proficiency in the doctrine of the law."[50] The Jews could not hear the warnings

43. Calvin, *Commentaries on the Book of Genesis*, vol. 1, 436.

44. Calvin, *Commentaries on the Epistle of Paul to the Romans*, 377.

45. Calvin, *Commentaries on the Epistle of Paul to the Romans*, 383.

46. Calvin, *Sermons on Genesis*, 550.

47. Calvin, *Commentary on the First Epistle of Paul to the Corinthians*, 86.

48. Calvin, *Commentary on the First Epistle of Paul to the Corinthians*, 87.

49. Calvin, *Commentary upon the Acts of the Apostles*, vol. 2, 144.

50. Calvin, *Commentary on the Second Epistle of Paul to the Corinthians*, 182–83.

given by the prophets. "Jeremiah spent his labour among them in vain, for he addressed the deaf, or rather stocks and stones, for they were so possessed by stupor that they understood nothing, for God had even blinded them, a judgment which they fully deserved."[51] "They had a veil over their eyes, so that they did not see Christ in the Law."[52] It was because of their darkened hearts that "Christ" was "not acknowledged by the chosen people." "The Jews," in fact, "obstinately rejected Christ."[53] Calvin wrote about the folly of Jerusalem referring to "the monstrous stupidity of that city, that, when God is present, it does not perceive him."[54]

The Church Is No Less Guilty

Calvin in expounding upon the biblical material regarding the sins of the Jews did not reflect an air of spiritual superiority.[55] Oberman observed, "For Calvin, Christians and Jews are so clearly the one People of God that the prophetic critique is a call for reform of the whole Church throughout all history and particularly in his own time."[56]

We find a call for repentance in a number of places in Calvin's writing. He concluded, for example, Lecture 44 on the prophecy of Daniel by acknowledging that he and the church of his time were no different than Israel in terms of their sin and the divine chastisement for it: "Grant, Almighty God, as at the present time thou dost deservedly chastise us for our sins, according to the example of thine ancient people, that we may turn our face to thee with true penitence and humility: May we throw ourselves suppliantly and

---

51. Calvin, *Commentaries on the Book of the Prophet Jeremiah and the Lamentations*, vol. 4, 5.

52. Calvin, *Commentaries on the First Epistle of Peter*, 47.

53. Calvin, *Commentary on the Second Epistle of Paul to the Corinthians*, 181.

54. Calvin, *Commentary on a Harmony of the Evangelists*, vol. 2, 455.

55. Pater affirms, "Calvin held that Christians had been *worse* idolaters than the Jews." Pater, "Calvin, the Jews and the Judaic Legacy," 271.

56. Oberman, "John Calvin: The Mystery of His Impact," 4.

prostrately before thee; and, despairing of ourselves, place our only hope in thy pity which thou hast promised us."[57] He maintained in Lecture 46 that "the impiety of this people was far greater than that of all others on account of their ingratitude, contumacy, and impracticable obstinacy." In fact, "the Israelites surpassed all nations in malice, ingratitude, and all kinds of iniquity." These facts, though, had a direct application to the church.[58] "Our impiety," he said, "is the more detestable to God the nearer he approaches us; and the kinder he is to us, the more chargeable we are, unless in our turn we prove ourselves grateful and obedient."[59]

We do not see an attitude of self-righteousness in Calvin as he contemplated the sins of the Jews as presented in the biblical canon. Calvin acknowledged that he too had broken the law of God. An implication for prayer followed from this fact. "We must remark in general the impossibility of our pleasing God by our prayers, unless we approach him as criminals, and repose all our hopes on his mercy."[60] Calvin thus offered this prayer: "Grant, Almighty God, that we may learn seriously to consider in how many ways we become guilty before thee, especially while we daily continue to provoke thy wrath against us." Sinners in the presence of God can only appeal to mercy: "May we be humbled by true and serious repentance, and fly eagerly to thee, as nothing is left to us but thy pity alone."[61] On another occasion, he prayed, "May the serious weight of our wickedness truly humble us when we come into thy sight, and call upon thee even from the lowest depths." Our only hope for acceptance with God, he acknowledged, is found in putting our trust in Christ: "And as thou hast granted us a Mediator who may procure favour for us from thee, may we never hesitate to approach thee familiarly, through reliance on him."[62]

57. Calvin, *Commentaries on the Book of the Prophet Daniel*, vol. 2, 145.

58. Oberman, *The Two Reformations*, 123.

59. Calvin, *Commentaries on the Book of the Prophet Daniel*, vol. 2, 167.

60. Calvin, *Commentaries on the Book of the Prophet Daniel*, vol. 2, 149.

61. Calvin, *Commentaries on the Book of the Prophet Daniel*, vol. 2, 169.

62. Calvin, *Commentaries on the Book of the Prophet Daniel*, vol. 2, 191.

Calvin understood that sin was not found in Israel alone. The church has sinned, and all the nations of the world have sinned. The same note is seen in the writing of David Torrance as he reflected upon the sin of the human race in renouncing Christ: "In a mysterious but nevertheless real way, the whole of humanity was involved in the rejection of Jesus. It was not just the self-righteousness of the religious leaders of the day" that "caused Jesus' death." "In one way or another 'we were there when they crucified the Lord,' as the song says."[63]

Our sin, Torrance contended, is not just connected to the past. He called attention to the spiritual condition of Israel and the entire world at the present time: "The great majority of Jews, either in the land of Israel or throughout the world, do not accept Jesus as Messiah and the majority remain, in some measure, agnostic."[64] At the same time, Torrance drew attention to the fact that the Gentile world is no different: "The other nations" are "just as sinful." In fact, "Israel's sin is the sin of the other nations, and the Church, alas, in her blindness has failed to help Israel to be the people of God." He added, "Her sin is our sin, and her rejection of God's call is our rejection of God's call to our obedience and love."[65]

Ongoing Spiritual Blindness

In his explanation of the prophet's confession of sin in Daniel 9:5, Calvin asserted that the Jews "had no pretext for their ignorance after they had been instructed in God's law." He compared them to "a man who stumbles in broad daylight." "The law of God was like a lamp pointing out the path" for them to walk in. But "they were willfully and even maliciously blind."[66] Their lack of spiritual perception, however, was not something that merely characterized the past. It was still the case, contended Calvin, when it came to

---

63. Torrance and Taylor, *Israel, God's Servant*, 124.

64. Torrance, "Israel Today, in the Light of God's Word," 109.

65. Torrance, "Israel Today, in the Light of God's Word," 110.

66. Calvin, *Commentaries on the Book of the Prophet Daniel*, vol. 2, 151.

their ongoing engagement with the biblical text.[67] Calvin would at times express his frustration with rabbinic exegesis and the inability of the Jews to understand biblical truth. They could not, for example, understand the statement in Genesis 15:6 concerning Abram: "And he believed in the LORD, and He accounted it to him for righteousness." Calvin told his congregants, "The Jews also are so blind and stupid that they do not know what this means." They "have a veil before them, as Paul says." "So they pass over these words without thinking about their importance."[68]

In his exposition of Acts 7 and the address of Stephen before the Sanhedrin, Calvin declared, "The Jews have always been wicked interpreters of the law, because they conceived nothing but that which was earthly."[69] We see a similar thing in his commentary on Daniel 7:27.[70] He said, "Since their object is the adulteration of sound doctrine, God also blinds them till they become utterly in the dark, and both trifling and childish; and if I were to stop to refute their crudities, I should never come to an end."[71] In his reflections on Psalm 136:13, Calvin attributed the "corrupting" of "the Scriptures" with "vain fancies" by some "Rabbinical writers" who "were led to this by the devil, as an artful way of discrediting the Scriptures."[72]

The spiritual blindness of the Jews resulted in their ongoing rejection of Jesus as the Messiah. Zwingli had made the same point declaring that the Jews "sin for not accepting the Lord Jesus as the Christ."[73] Calvin concurred. Commenting on Genesis 49:10, a passage that links the scepter with the tribe of Judah, Calvin declared

67. Blacketer, "Calvin As Commentator on the Mosaic Harmony and Joshua," 33.

68. Calvin, *Sermons on Genesis*, 315.

69. Calvin, *Commentary upon the Acts of the Apostles*, vol. 1, 306.

70. Many of Calvin's commentaries on the prophets were the result of his students transcribing his lectures given in the Academy in Geneva. Wilcox, "Calvin As Commentator on the Prophets," 107.

71. Calvin, *Commentaries on the Book of the Prophet Daniel*, vol. 2, 72.

72. Calvin, *Commentary on the Book of Psalms*, vol. 5, 186.

73. Gordon, *Zwingli*, 120.

that the Jews "endeavoured to envelop" the text "in clouds" and refused "to run to embrace" the Messiah promised in the passage. "They purposely," he said, "catch at every possible subterfuge, by which they may lead themselves and others far astray in tortuous by-paths."[74] They were, he said, no different than their ancestors in the first century: "The Jews turn away their eyes as much as they can from Christ."[75]

There is no question that Calvin could make jarring statements about his theological opponents. Appealing to passages such as Titus 1:9, Calvin believed that pastors "have a charge from God to uphold the truth and to defend it against all attacks."[76] "We should not therefore," he said, "think it odd if pastors speak roughly from the pulpit and appear excessively strict and severe."[77] His invectives were often directed against the Roman Catholic church.[78] In his defense of the biblical legitimacy of marriage for pastors, for example, Calvin denounced the demand of the papacy for clerical celibacy. He referred to "these papal scum and riff-raff," "the pope and all his lackeys," and "that devil in Rome" who "spews out his infernal blasphemy by declaring that those who are married cannot please God!"[79] "Among the papists," he declared, "we observe the worst possible confusion." "They are without discernment." "They would be happy to turn men into idiots, for to believe as they do one would have to abandon all reason and common sense."[80]

The Jews in their opposition to Christianity, no less than the religion of Rome, were not immune to Calvin's lightning bolts. In his lecture on Daniel 2:44–45, he declared, "I have had much conversation with many Jews: I have never seen either a drop of piety or a grain of truth or ingenuousness—nay, I have never found

74. Calvin, *Commentaries on the Book of Genesis*, vol. 2, 452.

75. Calvin, *Commentary on the Second Epistle of Paul to the Corinthians*, 183.

76. Calvin, *Sermons on Titus*, 94.

77. Calvin, *Sermons on Titus*, 98.

78. Pater, "Calvin, the Jews and the Judaic Legacy," 288.

79. Calvin, *Sermons on Titus*, 62.

80. Calvin, *Sermons on Titus*, 90.

common sense in any Jew."[81] This was a different tone than that of Johannes Reuchlin who referred to the rabbi who had taught him Hebrew, Jacob ben Jehiel Loans (d. 1506), as "my most humane teacher, the excellent doctor."[82] Reuchlin in a letter to his beloved teacher referred to him as "My Lord, dear master Jacob, my companion, and my good friend." He then expressed his friendship with him: "With deep longing I wish to see your blessed face to delight in the radiance of your bright countenance by hearing your most pure doctrine."[83] This statement was not to suggest that Reuchlin believed that Judaism contained the full truth. Reuchlin accepted Jesus as the Messiah, and the Jewish religion did not. Judaism did, however, in the view of Reuchlin, have some grains of truth, and he was willing to acknowledge that fact.[84]

Appreciation of Rabbinic Interpretation

We do not find Calvin linking any rabbi with pure doctrine.[85] He could, nevertheless, make positive statements regarding rabbinic interpretation.[86] He reflected the sixteenth-century "Christian love affair" with Hebrew and Jewish perspectives on the biblical text.[87] In Calvin's commentary on Psalm 112:5, for example, he referred to the thirteenth century Old Testament Jewish exegete David Kimchi (1160–1235) calling him "the most correct expositor among the Rabbins."[88] In Lecture 48 on the book of Daniel,

81. Calvin, *Commentaries on the Book of the Prophet Daniel*, vol. 1, 185.

82. Price, *Johannes Reuchlin*, 65.

83. Price, *Johannes Reuchlin*, 61.

84. Price, *Johannes Reuchlin*, 227.

85. Thompson contends that "Calvin's knowledge of rabbinic writings was not obtained directly but derived most often from annotations in Sebastian Münster's *Biblia Hebraica*, which summarized rabbinic arguments in Latin." Thompson, "Calvin As a Biblical Interpreter," 65.

86. Zachman, "Calvin As Commentator on Genesis," 18–19.

87. Cooper, "Christian Hebraism in the Renaissance and Reformation," 186.

88. Calvin, *Commentary on the Book of Psalms*, vol. 4, 326. Cf., Balserak,

Calvin interpreted the phrase "for the Lord's sake" in Daniel 9:17 as being a reference to the Mediator between God and man. He acknowledged that "all the Hebrew doctors agree" that the word "*Adoni*" is a reference to "God alone." Calvin, though, dissented from this interpretation maintaining that the prophet "sets before God the Mediator by whose favor he hopes to obtain his request." At the same time, though, he had no problem in affirming that students of the biblical text might well prefer the rabbinic view of the passage.[89] "Still, if any one prefers to apply this to God," said Calvin, "let him retain his opinion."[90]

In Calvin's commentary work in the Psalms, he frequently paid attention to Jewish exegetes as he wrestled with the interpretation of the biblical text.[91] His overall approach in interacting with rabbinic interpretation of the Old Testament irritated the Lutheran theologian Aegidius Hunnius (1550–1603). He censured Calvin for his dependence on Jewish scholarship in his book *The Judaizing Calvin.*[92] In the view of Hunnius, Calvin approached the Old Testament as a Hebrew Bible, not as Christian Scripture. Calvin in his judgment was too inclined to jettison patristic exegesis with its strong Christological readings of Old Testament passages.[93] This approach also annoyed the Lutheran Georg Nigrinus (1530–1602) who reproached Calvin for interpreting, in his judgment, "many important passages in the Old Testament, just as the rabbis interpret them."[94]

Calvin, however, reflected the same outlook as some of his Protestant contemporaries who consulted Jewish biblical commentaries.[95] Zwingli utilized the rabbinic linguistic insights of

---

Establishing the Remnant Church in France, 151.

89. Puckett, *John Calvin's Exegesis of the Old Testament*, 53.

90. Calvin, *Commentaries on the Book of the Prophet Daniel*, vol. 2, 181.

91. De Greef, "Calvin As Commentator on the Psalms," 106.

92. Austin, *The Jews and the Reformation*, 147–48.

93. Steinmetz, "John Calvin and the Jews," 391–92.

94. Detmers, "Calvin, the Jews, and Judaism," 198.

95. Austin notes that the Puritans were frequently accused of Judaizing because of their enthusiasm for the Old Testament. Austin, *The Jews and the*

David Kimchi, while Martin Bucer worked not only with Kimchi, but also with Abraham Ibn Ezra (1092–1167) and Rashi of Troyes (1040–1105) as sources in his commentary on the Psalms.[96] Calvin had a warm friendship with Konrad Pellikan (1478–1556), professor of Hebrew and Greek in Zurich.[97] Pellikan produced the first printed Hebrew lexicon and translated rabbinic texts.[98] Wolfgang Musculus (1497–1563) spoke in a positive way about Kimchi and the twelfth-century Jewish biblical commentator Abraham Ibn Ezra.[99] A similar admiration for aspects of Jewish interpretation is seen in the Lutheran theologian and Hebraist Andreas Osiander (1498–1552).[100] He affirmed, "It is undeniable that the Jews understand the Law and the Prophets better than Christians, except that they do not hold Christ to be the person we understand him to be."[101] We find the same thing in Sebastian Münster (1488–1552) who served as professor of Hebrew at the University of Basel.[102] Münster provided a Latin translation for the Bomberg Hebrew Bible along with annotations that reflected rabbinic exegesis.[103] Martin Luther (1483–1546) criticized him for his appreciation of Jewish exegetical insights, but Calvin remained on good terms with him and appears to have studied Hebrew with Münster.[104]

Reformation, 194.

96. Pak affirms, "Bucer explicitly uses Jewish exegesis and finds great value in it as a tool for Christian exegesis." Pak, *The Judaizing* Calvin, 11–12. Cf., Austin, *The Jews and the Reformation*, 74, 93; Hobbs, "Bucer, the Jews, and Judaism," 149–52.

97. Balserak, *John Calvin as Sixteenth-Century Prophet*, 34.

98. Gordon, *Zwingli*, 144; Kirn, "Ulrich Zwingli, the Jews, and Judaism," 174.

99. De Greef, "Calvin As Commentator on the Psalms," 90.

100. Gritsch, "The Jews in Reformation Theology," 201; Kammerling, "Andreas Osiander's Sermons on the Jews," 63; Pater, "Calvin, the Jews and the Judaic Legacy," 261.

101. Kammerling, "Andreas Osiander, the Jews, and Judaism," 228.

102. Münster translated the Gospel of Matthew into Hebrew and published it in 1537. Austin, *From Judaism to Calvinism*, 76.

103. Austin, *The Jews and the Reformation*, 153.

104. Gordon, *Calvin*, 51; De Greef, *Of One Tree*, 72. Puckett maintains that Calvin may also have drawn upon the expertise of Wolfgang Capito in his

Learning from the Jews

Thomas Torrance in recent years expressed appreciation for Jewish insights into the meaning of the biblical text.[105] He observed that we Gentiles "fail again and again" in our "quest of the historical Jesus." He concluded, "All we seem finally to do is to construct a picture of Jesus which fits into our own western cultural preconceptions." The end result is disastrous: "We put a Gentile mask on the face of Jesus which both obscures him from ourselves and prevents our Jewish brethren from recognizing in the Jesus of Christianity" the "Christ who is their own covenanted Messiah." If we would understand who "he really was and is" we must have "the help of our brethren the Jews themselves." Torrance then noted that he had once worked with a Jewish scholar who could discern things in the New Testament which he could not see.[106] Torrance argued that he needed to remove his Gentile spectacles which distorted what was in the biblical text. There are times, said Torrance, when "we need to go to school with the People of Israel, as it were, in order to share with them the training they were given by God through many, many centuries."[107]

Calvin along with Augustine of Hippo (354–430) recognized that the Jewish diaspora in divine providence had a beneficial side to it. Augustine in speaking about "the Hebrew people" had said that "this people was scattered among the nations to bear witness to the Scriptures, which foretold the coming of Christ." "The ceremonies, the priesthoods, the tabernacle or the temple, the altars,

---

study of Hebrew. Puckett, *John Calvin's Exegesis of the Old Testament*, 58.

105. De Greef makes the point that in the thinking of Calvin there must be "a readiness on our part to be instructed" by the Jews. "The work of the Holy Spirit" in the view of Calvin meant that the Spirit "renews people in such a way that they willingly let themselves be taught by the Jews." De Greef, *Of One Tree*, 90.

106. Torrance and Taylor provide this exhortation: "Members of the mainstream churches need to listen to Messianic Believers and learn from them." Torrance and Taylor, *Israel, God's Servant*, 7.

107. Torrance, "The Divine Vocation and Destiny of Israel in World History," 97.

the sacrifices, the sacred rites, the festal days, and everything which is concerned with the homage due to God . . . all these were symbols and predictions that find fulfillment in Christ, so as to give eternal life to those who believe."[108] Calvin had the same perspective. "We must know," he said, "that whither soever the Jews were exiled, there went with them some seed of godliness, and there was some smell [savour] of pure doctrine spread abroad." Commenting on the presence of Gentile God-fearers in the synagogues that were spread throughout the Mediterranean world, Calvin affirmed, "Their miserable scattering abroad was so turned unto a contrary end by the wonderful counsel of God, that it did gather those unto the true faith who did wander in error." There were at least some Gentiles who left full-scale paganism and were "enticed unto Judaism" with its commitment to monotheism, "the worship of one and the true God."[109] He also insisted that Jewish blindness would not continue forever. "Paul teaches us," he said, "that they were thus blinded for a time by God's providence, that a way to the gospel might be made for the Gentiles, and that still they were not for ever excluded from the favour of God."[110]

The Ultimate Wickedness

Jewish unbelief had tragic consequences for generations to come, but history could not be undone. They did what they did and killed the Messiah. This had been prophesied in the Old Testament. Zechariah 12:10 had announced that the time would come when they would look upon him whom they had pierced and would mourn for him as one mourns for an only son. "God," stated Calvin, "had not only been formerly provoked in a disgraceful manner by the Jews, but that at length in the person of his only-begotten Son this great sin was added to their disgraceful impiety, that they pierced the side of Christ." "It is indeed true," he acknowledged, "that

108. Augustine, *Concerning the City of God*, 293.

109. Calvin, *Commentary upon the Acts of the Apostles*, vol. 2, 133.

110. Calvin, *Commentaries on the Epistle of Paul the Apostle to the Romans*, 440.

the side of Christ was pierced by a Roman soldier, but, as Peter says, he was crucified by the Jews, for they were the authors of his death, and Pilate was almost forced by them to condemn him."[111] What happened to Jesus fit a long-established pattern. "Jerusalem" had "been long accustomed to suck the blood of the prophets." "It was not wonderful if a city, which had been accustomed to strangle or stone *the prophets*, should cruelly put to death its own Redeemer."[112] The one who came to bring healing was slaughtered by them: "They wrecked their cruelty on the Physician himself."[113]

How evil was the Jewish rejection of the Messiah? Increase Mather reflected on the same issue in the seventeenth century: "For what guilt can there be greater than the guilt which lyeth upon the miserable Nation of the *Jews*?"[114] He answered his own question: "It is certain, that the most prodigious Murther that ever the Sun beheld, (yea such Murther as the Son duest not behold) hath been committed by the *Jews*, and that the guilt thereof lyeth upon the Jewish nation to this day, even the guilt of the blood of the Saviour of the world."[115]

Barth spoke about the relative guilt of Gentiles and Jews in what happened to Christ: "The passion of the Son of Man is, of course, the work of the Gentiles, of Pilate and his race, but only secondarily and incidentally." "It is not the case" that "Israel and the Gentiles, Church and state, cooperated equally in accusing and condemning Jesus and destroying Him as a criminal." Rather, "it is Israel, represented by its spiritual and ecclesiastical and theological leaders, but also by its *vox populi* that refuses and rejects and condemns Jesus and finally delivers Him up as a blasphemer to the Gentiles."[116]

Thomas Torrance of the Church of Scotland commented upon Israel's rejection of Christ, "condemning him to a sinner's

111. Calvin, *Commentaries on the Prophet Zechariah*, 364–65.
112. Calvin, *Commentary on a Harmony of the Evangelists*, vol. 3, 105–6.
113. Calvin, *Commentary on a Harmony of the Evangelists*, vol. 3, 136.
114. Mather, *The Mystery of Israel's Salvation*, 172.
115. Mather, *The Mystery of Israel's Salvation*, 175–76.
116. Barth, *Church Dogmatics*, vol. 4, part 2, 260.

death." "The Jews," he said, "carried that out in fearful wickedness, in the ultimate refusal of grace." Indeed, they "became guilty of the ultimate wickedness of putting the Son of God to death."[117] Calvin had given a similar assessment: "No words can express the baseness of their criminality in putting to death the Son of God, who had been sent to them as the Author of life." "The rejection of Christ" was "worthy of abhorrence above all the sins committed in all ages."[118]

David Torrance remarked, "In the crucifying of Jesus all sin boiled over. This was the most desperate act of wickedness where man in his freedom rose up in revolt against God and tried to destroy him." Torrance here reflected a long-standing perspective in Reformed theology, but he reminded us that there is more to the story: "God took this same most sinful act of man, over-ruled it, and by Grace, made it his saving act for the world." "So man's very rejection of Christ at the cross, by God's over-ruling grace, is made to perfect God's redemption of man and to work for God's glory."[119]

Dreadful Divine Vengeance

There, nevertheless, would be terrible consequences for what the Jews had done. When Pilate in his judicial capacity declared that he was innocent of the blood of Jesus, the Jews persisted in their demand that Jesus be crucified and pronounced in Matthew 27:25 a curse upon themselves affirming that his blood would be upon them and their children. "Their impiety," said Calvin, was such that God "justly revenged it by dreadful and unusual methods."[120] John Chrysostom in the fourth century had taken the same position asking the question: "Whence came there thus upon them wrath from God intolerable, and more sore than all that had befallen aforetime, not in Judæa only, but in any part of the world? Is

---

117. Torrance, *Incarnation*, 53.

118. Calvin, *Commentary on a Harmony of the Evangelists*, vol. 3, 1367

119. Torrance, "The Witness of the Jews to God," 6.

120. Calvin, *Commentary on a Harmony of the Evangelists*, vol. 3, 289.

it not quite clear, that it was for the deed of the cross, and for this rejection?" He assessed their rejection of Christ by asserting, "For neither had any man perpetrated, not of those that ever have been, nor of those to come hereafter, a deed so wicked and horrible."[121] Calvin made the point that there would be consequences for their actions: "God determined" to "take vengeance on that nation, for having rejected his Son, and despised the grace which was brought by him."[122] "Jerusalem will suffer dreadful punishment," Calvin noted, "because she despised the Redeemer who had been exhibited to her, and did not embrace his grace."[123]

The great wonder is that the vengeance of God upon his covenant people is not the final message of the biblical revelation. Calvin and the mainstream Reformed tradition understood that the Jews as a people are forever loved by God and will eventually come to salvation as a nation in the time of the divine appointment. We now turn out attention to the incredible reality that although they are cast aside, it will not be forever.

121. Chrysostom, "Homilies on the Gospel of Saint Matthew," 457.

122. Calvin, *Commentary on a Harmony of the Evangelists*, vol. 3, 116.

123. Calvin, *Commentary on a Harmony of the Evangelists*, vol. 2, 456.

4

Cast Aside, But Not Forever

"GOD PROMISED TO THE seed of Abraham that he would be their God." This was Calvin's position. He maintained, though, that the promise of salvation necessitated the embrace of faith. Indeed, there was always a remnant of believers in the midst of Israel even in the darkest days, but the nation as a whole at the time of Christ was guilty of the crime of unbelief. What would follow as a result of their lack of faith? "All unbelievers," affirmed Calvin, "by rejecting this promise, excluded themselves from the family of *Abraham*."[1] "The Jews conducted themselves proudly and insolently toward God, as if they had been elected through their own merit. On account of their ingratitude and insolence the Lord rejects them as unworthy."[2] Reflecting upon the figure of the olive tree employed by Paul in Romans 11, Calvin noted that Paul maintains that *some* of the Jewish branches were broken off from the tree: "Paul wisely mitigates the severity of the case, by not saying that the whole top of the tree was cut off, but that some of the branches were broken, and also that God took some here and there from among the Gentiles, whom he set in the holy and blessed trunk."[3]

1. Calvin, *Commentary on the Gospel according to John*, vol. 1, 347.
2. Calvin, *Commentary on the Book of the Prophet Isaiah*, vol. 4, 378.
3. Calvin, *Commentaries on the Epistle of Paul the Apostle to the Romans*, 428.

Blessing for the Nations

Calvin commented on the remarkable turn of events that began to be played out already in the first century: "The fall of the Jews had turned out for salvation to the Gentiles."[4] "God had in a manner so blinded Israel, that while they refused the light of the gospel, it might be transferred to the Gentiles, and that these might occupy, as it were, the vacated possession."[5] The teaching of the apostle in Romans 11 was a repetition of what Jesus had prophesied in Matthew 8:11–12 as he marveled at the faith of the centurion declaring that Gentiles would sit down with the patriarchs in the kingdom of heaven, even while the Jews in unbelief would be cast into outer darkness. Calvin reflecting upon this passage affirmed, "That the Gentiles should be admitted, by a free adoption, into the same body with the posterity of Abraham, could scarcely be endured: but that the Jews themselves should be driven out, to make way for their being succeeded by the Gentiles, appeared to them altogether monstrous." Calvin added, "Yet Christ declares that both will happen: that God will admit strangers into the bosom of Abraham, and that he will exclude the *children*."[6]

Calvin drew the attention of the church in Geneva to the successive reduction and growth of the offspring of Abraham. He asserted, "God diminishes that seed in order to increase it." On the one hand, "when there is seed, there is a large number, an astonishing multitude, but God cuts it back, God reduces it, diminishes it, so that is sometimes seems that it is almost all consumed" and "almost nothing is left to be seen." But then God seems to change course: "He does that to multiply it later above human imagination." The dividing line was the entrance of Christ, the Son of God, into the world. "For even though many peoples descended from Abraham, the twelve lines in the first case, and then the Ishmaelites

---

4. Calvin, *Commentaries on the Epistle of Paul the Apostle to the Romans*, 421.

5. Calvin, *Commentaries on the Epistle of Paul the Apostle to the Romans*, 436.

6. Calvin, *Commentary on a Harmony of the Evangelists*, vol. 1, 383.

and Idumeans, the fact is that there was never a multitude so great in his house as it has been through our Lord Jesus Christ." What happened? "Those who have no attachment to Abraham according to the flesh were made his servants, for he was, as we will see later, the father of all believers in general."[7]

Salvific blessing in the view of Calvin would still have come to the Gentile world even if the Jews had not fallen into unbelief. "If the Jews had continued faithful," he said, "the Gentiles would have been joined with them, as it has been said, 'In those days it shall come to pass that ten men shall take hold of the skirt of him that is a Jew,' (Zech. viii.23;) but their rebellion brought it about, that God only gathered from them the first-fruits of His church, and afterwards the Gentiles were substituted in the place which they had left empty."[8]

The incorporation of believing Gentiles into the body of Christ and the salvation that came to them was the fulfillment of ancient promises given to Abraham. There was the declaration of the Lord in Genesis 12:3 that in him all the families of the earth would be blessed. This, Calvin believed, was a divine commitment of fundamental significance: "On one great promise made to Abraham all the others hang, and without it they lose all their value: 'In thy seed shall the nations of the earth be blessed.'"[9] The importance of this promise was due to the fact that it drew attention to the coming Messiah. God "pronounces that all nations should be blessed in his servant Abram, because Christ was included in his loins."[10]

A Father of Many Nations

There was also the promise of the Lord in Genesis that Abraham would be a father of many nations. It is true that different nations had their origin from the holy patriarch, but this pledge included

7. Calvin, *Sermons on Genesis*, 312.
8. Calvin, *Commentaries on the Last Four Books of Moses*, vol. 1, 409.
9. Calvin, *Commentaries on the Epistle of Paul to the Ephesians*, 233.
10. Calvin, *Sermons on Genesis*, 71.

more than his biological offspring.[11] Abraham, as Paul states in Romans 4:11, would be the father of all who believe. As Cotton Mather put it, "Not only all the *Jewish*, but now all the *Christian* World, speak of *Abraham*, in that Style, *Our Father Abraham*."[12] Calvin likewise wrote, "The Gentiles were to be, by faith, inserted into the stock of Abram, although not descended from him according to the flesh."

The believing nations are given a remarkable status. In his exposition of Genesis 17:4–8, Calvin declared, "We cannot enter the church and be considered among the faithful if we are not made one with this ancient people."[13] He proclaimed the same idea in a sermon on 2 Samuel 7:22–24: "Although we are not descended from the race of Abraham, though God has not brought us back from the land of Egypt, still we have been associated with these people who were elected and chosen."[14] How does this happen?[15] "This is not done according to the flesh, but by faith. God has created such a union among us that we are made children of Abraham."[16] Gentile believers have been given a remarkable privilege. Calvin instructed his congregation, "Today we follow in the place of Abraham's children, having been grafted into their place," "we who were like wild plants and useless trees." "We have the bond and place of honour that belonged to the ancient Jews."[17]

11. Torrance and Taylor comment, "Gentiles too were brought to the Messiah, and so became spiritual descendants of Abraham." "Though they were not physically circumcised, they became what Paul calls 'the circumcision.'" Torrance and Taylor, *Israel, God's Servant*, 127.

12. Mather, *Genesis*, 914.

13. Calvin, *Sermons on Genesis*, 545.

14. Calvin, *Sermons on 2 Samuel*, 381.

15. De Greef, "Calvin As Commentator on the Psalms," 95.

16. Calvin, *Sermons on Genesis*, 545.

17. Calvin, *Sermons on Genesis*, 549.

Grace for the Children

Calvin in continuity with Bullinger believed that the genealogical embrace of the Abrahamic covenant continues into the present day.[18] It includes Jews and is a blessing that is applied to believing Gentiles.[19] The salvific favor of the Lord in Calvin's exegesis is generational: "He wishes to extend his grace and increase it among us and even continue it from children to children for a thousand generations."[20] Reflecting upon the statement in Psalm 103:17 that the righteousness of the Lord stretches forth to children's children, Calvin wrote, "It is a singular proof of his love that he not only receives each of us individually into his favour, but also herein associates with us our offspring, as it were by hereditary right, that they may be partakers of the same adoption."[21] He comforted his flock, "God still validates what he once said, that he will be the God and Father of those he sanctified unto himself." "He extends his grace, his goodness and mercy to the children of the children from age to age."[22] He brought this exhortation: "Let fathers who have children and hear that promise bless God doubly and magnify him for not being content to receive them for himself but for also wanting to include their children in that promise."[23]

New Testament texts that Calvin appealed to in support of his position that God continues to pour out his generational grace in the period of the new covenant include Acts 2:39 in which Peter declared that the promise of the Holy Spirit was for the Jews and their children. The adjoining of the children with their believing parents was due to "the words of the promise" given to

---

18. Bullinger, "The One and Eternal Testament or Covenant of God," 107.

19. De Greef reflects on Calvin's emphasis on the unity of the covenant: "The covenant that God made with the fathers, he says, differs not at all in substance and reality from his covenant with us, but in fact they are one and the same." De Greef, "Calvin As Commentator on the Psalms," 105.

20. Calvin, *Sermons on Genesis*, 558.

21. Calvin, *Commentary on the Book of Psalms*, vol. 4, 139.

22. Calvin, *Sermons on Genesis*, 559.

23. Calvin, *Sermons on Genesis*, 559–60.

Abraham "I will be thy God, and the God of thy seed after thee."[24] "Peter teacheth," said Calvin, "that all the children of the Jews are contained in the same covenant, because this promise is always in force, I will be the God of your seed."[25] The salvation of the household of Cornelius described in Acts 10 demonstrates that the Abrahamic covenant was not restricted to Jews. "The Gentiles" were "adopted together into the society of the covenant."[26] Are Gentile children likewise embraced by the covenant in the era of the New Testament church? Calvin answered, "The children of the faithful which are born in the Church are from their mother's womb of the household of the kingdom of God."[27]

The Children Are Holy

Calvin saw enormous significance in the statement of Paul in 1 Corinthians 7:14 that the unbelieving spouse in a marriage is sanctified by the husband or the wife who is a believer. In addition, any children of the marriage were in fact holy. "The passage," commented Calvin, "is a remarkable one, and drawn from the depths of theology; for it teaches, that the children of the pious are set apart from others by a sort of exclusive privilege, so as to be reckoned *holy* in the Church." What was the basis of this unusual blessing? Calvin at this point reminded his readers of the Abrahamic covenant: "As to the Apostle's assigning here a peculiar privilege to the children of believers, this flows from the blessing of the covenant." Paul's declaration in Romans 11:16 is significant. "*If the root be holy,* says he, *then the branches are holy also.*" Said Calvin, "The whole of Abraham's posterity are holy, because God had made a covenant of life with him." It must be understood that "the same covenant of salvation that was entered into with the seed

---

24. Calvin, *Commentary upon the Acts of the Apostles*, vol. 1, 122.
25. Calvin, *Commentary upon the Acts of the Apostles*, vol. 1, 123.
26. Calvin, *Commentary upon the Acts of the Apostles*, vol. 1, 451.
27. Calvin, *Commentary upon the Acts of the Apostles*, vol. 1, 454.

of Abraham is communicated to us." Thus "the children of believers" are "set apart to the Lord."[28]

John Frame and others in our time argue, as Calvin did, in favor of the ongoing generational embrace of the divine covenants. "In salvation," states Frame, "God calls not only individuals, but families, households, even nations." This was true of the Noahic covenant, which was a covenant with Noah and his family. It was true of the Abrahamic covenant, "indicated by God's command to Abraham to circumcise all the males in his household." It is true, says Frame, of the new covenant. Peter on the day of Pentecost announces to Israel that the promise is for them and their children—Acts 2:39. Frame thus concludes that in the new covenant "God is calling families, and explicitly children," pointing out that "conversions in the NT are commonly of household units (Acts 11:14; 16:15, 31–34; 1 Cor. 1:16)."[29] Robert Letham makes a similar observation.[30] He reasons as follows: "If the children of believers were excluded from membership in the new covenant when they had been an integral part of the old covenant, Pentecost would have been a day of mass excommunication."[31]

Frame likewise, as Calvin did, draws attention to 1 Corinthians 7:14 and notes that "children, even in a marriage in which only one parent is a believer, are holy, that is, they belong to God."[32] Van Genderen and Velema reason in a similar way, stating, "God is the God of believers and their children." Referring to Genesis 17, they note that "God is the God of Abraham and his entire household."[33] Appealing to such passages as Acts 2:39, 1 Corinthians 7:14, and Ephesians 6:1, they affirm that children of believers "are also

28. Calvin, *Commentary on the First Epistle of Paul to the Corinthians*, 243.

29. Frame, *Systematic Theology*, 104.

30. Robert Letham has taught at several Reformed seminaries, most recently serving as Professor of Systematic and Historical Theology at Union School of Theology in Bridgend, Wales.

31. Letham, *Systematic Theology*, 445–46.

32. Frame, *Systematic Theology*, 1066.

33. Van Genderen and Velema, *Concise Reformed Dogmatics*, 563.

included in the church of the New Testament." Indeed, "they form a part of the holy people of God to whom the promises apply."[34]

The Abrahamic Covenant Endures Forever

Unproductive branches were broken off from the olive tree of grace and privilege. Calvin remarked, "When the people, through false zeal, had rejected the righteousness of God, they suffered a just punishment for their presumption, were deservedly blinded, and were at last cut off from the covenant."[35] This did not mean, though, that the promises made to Abraham and his biological descendants have been revoked, or that the church has replaced Israel.[36] Calvin distanced himself from the biblical exegesis of Christians who would disinherit the Jews and maintain that the promises of God no longer apply to them.[37] We must not "think," wrote Calvin, "that the covenant formerly made with Abraham is now abrogated." "The covenant which God made formerly with the fathers" has not been repealed. It "stands firm and inviolable."[38]

"I am that God, says he, who led you out of Egypt." For Calvin this often repeated statement in the Old Testament had great significance: "When God led his people out of Egypt, he did not set before them any momentary benefit." Rather, "he bore witness to the adoption of the race of Abraham on the condition of his being their perpetual Saviour." The redemption from Egypt had permanent implications: "He then received his people under his care on the very ground of never ceasing to act towards them with the love and anxiety of a father."[39] It is true that the Jews were cast aside,

---

34. Van Genderen and Velema, *Concise Reformed Dogmatics*, 697.

35. Calvin, *Commentaries on the Epistle of Paul to the Romans*, 409.

36. Klempa underscores the fact that Calvin maintained that in the church "the Jews have chief place." In Calvin's teaching, "the church has not replaced Israel." Klempa, "The First-Born in God's Family," 9. Cf., Venema, *The Promise of the Future*, 128.

37. Pak, *The Judaizing Calvin*, 10.

38. Calvin, *Commentaries on the Epistle of Paul to the Romans*, 409.

39. Calvin, *Commentaries on the Book of the Prophet Daniel*, vol. 2, 175.

but not forever.[40] The favor of God still rested upon them. Calvin affirmed, "By their ungratefulness they were forsaken as unworthy—yet forsaken in such a way that the heavenly blessing had not departed utterly from that nation. For this reason, despite their stubbornness and covenant-breaking, Paul still calls them holy."[41]

The language of Genesis 17:7 for Calvin had crucial significance. The covenant between the Lord and Abraham and his seed was generational and was everlasting in duration. "I grant, indeed," said Calvin, "that the covenant was without end, and may with propriety be called eternal."[42] "The purpose of God stands firm and immovable, by which he had deigned to choose them for himself as a peculiar nation." He reasoned, "Since then it cannot possibly be, that the Lord will depart from that covenant which he made with Abraham, 'I will be the God of thy seed,' (Gen. xvii.7,) it is evident that he has not wholly turned away his kindness from the Jewish nation."[43] "They have been," he said, "God's people from the beginning, that is, ever since he had entered into an inviolable covenant with Abraham."[44] Believers have always seen great significance in the words of the divine commitment revealed to Abraham: "The faithful take for granted that God had promised to the fathers that his covenant would be perpetual; for he did not only say to Abraham, 'I will be thy God,' but he also added, 'and of thy seed for ever.'" "They knew that God not only promised, but that having interposed an oath, by which God designed to confirm that covenant, that it might be unhesitatingly received by the chosen people." "The faithful knew that God in a manner bound himself to them."[45]

40. Van Genderen and Velema, *Concise Reformed Dogmatics*, 856.

41. Calvin, *Institutes of the Christian Religion*, vol. 2, 1336.

42. Calvin, *Commentaries on the Book of Genesis*, vol. 1, 450.

43. Calvin, *Commentaries on the Epistle of Paul to the Romans*, 441.

44. Calvin, *Commentary on the Book of Psalms*, vol. 3, 162.

45. Calvin, *Commentaries on the Prophet Micah*, 408.

The Return from Babylon

The irrevocable call of God had implications with respect to the question of the salvation of the Jewish people in the time to come. Calvin reminded his readers of the ongoing cycle chronicled in the Old Testament of chastisement followed by mercy. It was "an acknowledged axiom" that in Israel's past "God had so punished the unbelief of his people as not to forget his mercy." History demonstrated that the Lord had "often restored the Jews, after he had apparently banished them from his kingdom."[46] The Jews in exile would be in a "wretched and afflicted condition" in "Babylon, till at length God should have compassion on them and render assistance."[47] "The Lord, after having chastised his people, would at length shew mercy to them, so as to receive them into favour." "Their captivity would not be perpetual."[48] "They had been scattered as by a violent whirlwind like chaff or stubble; and God had so driven them away that there was no hope of being again gathered." "It was incredible, that a people so dispersed could be collected together" from "'all nations and from all places.'"[49]

Providing the reason for the divine promise in Isaiah 41:18 that the Lord would make the wilderness a pool of water, Calvin stated, "It was that the Jews might not think that they were prevented from returning to Judea by that vast desert in which travelers are scorched by the heat of the sun, and deprived of all the necessaries of life." "The Lord," he said, "therefore promises that he will supply them with water, and with everything else that is necessary for the journey." These promises "were fulfilled when the Lord brought his people out of Babylon."[50]

46. Calvin, *Commentaries on the Epistle of Paul to the Romans*, 434.

47. Calvin, *Commentary on the Book of the Prophet Isaiah*, vol. 3, 266.

48. Calvin, *Commentaries on the Book of the Prophet Jeremiah and the Lamentations*, vol. 4, 12.

49. Calvin, *Commentaries on the Book of the Prophet Jeremiah and the Lamentations*, vol. 3, 438.

50. Calvin, *Commentary on the Book of the Prophet Isaiah*, vol. 3, 267–68.

The Jews Shall Come to Salvation

The manifold mercies of God in bygone days would be continued to Israel in the ongoing course of history.[51] Calvin rejected the position that there was no future prospect for the salvation of the Jews.[52] Paul, he said, "asks the question" in Romans 11:11, "whether the Jewish nation had so stumbled at Christ, that it was all over with them universally, and that no hope of repentance remained." The text states, maintained Calvin, that "he justly denies that the salvation of the Jews was to be despaired of, or that they were so rejected by God, that there was no future restoration, or that the covenant of grace, which he had once made with them, was entirely abolished."[53]

A number of Reformed theologians in the sixteenth century insisted upon the future salvation of the Jews. One thinks here of Zwingli, Bucer, Vermigli, Beza, and Tremellius.[54] Huldrych Zwingli declared concerning the Jews, "God elected them from eternity, and he loved them more than others: thus for the sake of the fathers they are elect until now." "The fact that they are indeed the people of God for the sake of the fathers is plain." "That people will not be damned but will return to faith and be saved, even though they have been rejected for a time."[55] Martin Bucer affirmed, "When the fullness of the Gentiles has come to Christ, that is, the full number of the elect, all Israel also, that is, the entire nation, will be saved, and the kingdom of God will flourish once again among them."[56] Peter Martyr Vermigli (1499–1562) added, "The Jews have not so perished without exception that no hope

---

51. Venema, *The Promise of the Future*, 129.

52. Calvin anticipated, as De Greef affirms, that the Jews "will turn back from their apostasy. They will be reconciled with God and accept Jesus as the Messiah." De Greef, *Of One Tree*, 107.

53. Calvin, *Commentaries on the Epistle of Paul to the Romans*, 421.

54. Hesselink, "The Millennium in the Reformed Tradition," 101–2.

55. Shute, "*And All Israel Shall Be Saved*: Peter Martyr and John Calvin on the Jews," 164.

56. Shute, "*And All Israel Shall Be Saved*: Peter Martyr and John Calvin on the Jews," 165.

remains for their salvation. To this day remnants are preserved who are saved." "One day they will become a mighty band in full view."[57] Theodore Beza referred to "the holy nation of the Jews" and indicated that he offered petitions every day for them with all his heart: "Lord I pray that you will have regard for your covenant and look with kindly eyes on this forsaken and unfortunate people for your name's sake."[58] Immanuel Tremellius, a Jewish convert to Christianity, translated Calvin's Geneva Catechism into Hebrew and announced that he was awaiting the salvation of Israel.[59] He expressed his longing, "All my desires are for the redemption of Israel and therefore I have written this small book."[60]

Calvin was no exception in his expectation regarding the future.[61] He acknowledged that there had been "the defection of that people." Nevertheless, "the salvation of them all" was not "to be for ever despaired of," even though "a long delay tempts us to despair."[62] These are the days in which blindness in part has happened to Israel, and this will continue until the fullness of the Gentiles has come in. "When the Gentiles shall come in," maintained Calvin, "the Jews also shall return from their defection to the obedience of faith; and thus shall be completed the salvation of the whole Israel of God, which must be gathered from both; and yet in such a way that the Jews shall obtain the first place, being as it were the first-born in God's family."[63] Their turning to God would be a remarkable event. Indeed, "the mode of their conversion will

57. Shute, "*And All Israel Shall Be Saved*: Peter Martyr and John Calvin on the Jews," 166.

58. Austin, *The Jews and the Reformation*, 92.

59. The Hebraist Tremellius was also an expert in Syriac and produced both a Syriac grammar and translated the Syriac New Testament into Latin. Some scholars at the time believed that the Gospel of Matthew and the Epistle to the Hebrews were originally written in Syriac. Austin, *The Jews and the Reformation*, 154–55.

60. Austin, *The Jews and the Reformation*, 96.

61. Hesselink, "Calvin on the Relation of the Church and Israel," 105.

62. Calvin, *Commentaries on the Epistle of Paul to the Romans*, 435.

63. Calvin, *Commentaries on the Epistle of Paul to the Romans*, 437.

neither be common nor usual." "It will be incomprehensible until the time of its revelation."[64]

Our Attitude toward the Jews

Calvin noted that "Paul had such a high regard for the Jews, because he viewed them as bearing the character, and, as they commonly say, the quality of an elect people."[65] Such a perspective regarding the status of the Jews and their future salvation had implications for the attitude that Gentiles ought to have toward them.[66] Calvin sounded very much like the Strasbourg Reformer Wolfgang Capito at this point.[67] Capito stated, "We truly feel sorry for this people which has been despised for so long by everyone." Capito added, "We should also treat them honourably, insofar as they do not blaspheme against God, because they are descended from the holy race and were possessors of the promises and the covenants."[68]

Honor is to be given to the Jews and prayer is to be offered in their behalf. This is the case even though, as David Torrance observed, "Israel has not yet embraced Jesus as her Messiah." He raised the question, "Why do the mainstream churches of the West, almost without exception do little or nothing to take the Gospel to the Jews in Israel or throughout the world?"[69] He gave this exhortation: "We are called to pray with deep concern" that "they might recognize and accept the Living God, the Father of our Lord Jesus Christ, and submit to his way of salvation for them."[70] Letham likewise states, "Prayer for the effective reception of the gospel by the Jewish people worldwide is something close to the heart of

---

64. Calvin, *Commentaries on the Epistle of Paul to the Romans*, 435.

65. Calvin, *Commentaries on the Epistle of Paul to the Romans*, 337.

66. Gordon, *Calvin*, 117.

67. Desiderius Erasmus (ca. 1467–1536), in contrast to Calvin, hated the Jews. De Greef, *Of One Tree*, 50–51.

68. Austin, *The Jews and the Reformation*, 73.

69. Torrance and Taylor, *Israel, God's Servant*, 7.

70. Torrance, "Israel Today, in the Light of God's Word," 110.

God and should be made a priority."[71] Torrance and Letham stand in the tradition of Robert Murray M'Cheyne (1813–1843), a renowned minister in the Church of Scotland.[72] "The whole Bible," declared M'Cheyne, "shows that God has a peculiar affection for Israel."[73] He then asked, "Should we not give them the same place in our heart which God gives them in His heart?"[74]

The love which M'Cheyne had for the Jews was manifested in his missionary outreach to the Jews in 1839.[75] His biographer Andrew Bonar (1810–1892) noted that M'Cheyne had great facility in the Hebrew Bible: "He could consult the Hebrew original of the Old Testament with as much ease as most of our ministers are able to consult the Greek of the New."[76] It was the Hebrew text that M'Cheyne used in seeking to win the Jews to Christ. Bonar wrote concerning M'Cheyne's ministry on their missionary trip to Israel: "Mr. M'Cheyne's anxiety for souls appeared in the efforts he made to leave at least a few words of Scripture with the Jews whom he met." "With his Hebrew Bible in hand, he would walk up thoughtfully and solemnly to the first Jew he could get access to, and begin by calling the man's attention to some statement of God's word."[77] M'Cheyne himself testified, "We visited every town in the Holy Land where Jews are found." "The Hebrew Bible was produced, and passage after passage explained, none making us afraid."[78]

Calvin maintained that those who would mistreat the Jews should be condemned: "Those who abuse them acquire thereby

71. Letham, *Systematic Theology*, 841.

72. Torrance and Taylor observed, "The command to take the Gospel 'to the Jew first' and then to the Gentiles was cherished for many years by the Church of Scotland and from 1840 to 1960 the Church had two overseas missions, namely, 'Mission to the Jews' and 'Foreign Missions,' which covered wherever the Church was working throughout the rest of the world." Torrance and Taylor, *Israel, God's Servant*, 7–8.

73. Bonar, *Robert Murray M'Cheyne*, 492.

74. Bonar, *Robert Murray M'Cheyne*, 493.

75. Torrance, *The Reluctant Minister*, 305.

76. Bonar, *Robert Murray M'Cheyne*, 29.

77. Bonar, *Robert Murray M'Cheyne*, 109–10.

78. Bonar, *Robert Murray M'Cheyne*, 494.

nothing but a greater obloquy."[79] He further noted that Paul himself warned believers in Romans 11 about the sin of having a heart that is boastful and swollen with pride. It would be "unreasonable" for "the Gentiles to glory against the Jews, that is, with respect to the excellency of their race." The reason was that "the calling of the Gentiles was like an ingrafting, and that they did not otherwise grow up as God's people than as they were grafted in the stock of Abraham."[80] Paul was concerned "to check the arrogance of the Gentiles, that they should exult over the Jews."[81]

"The covenant which God had made once for all with the descendants of Abraham could in no way be made void." Calvin's summary of the biblical teaching meant that "Abraham's physical progeny must not be deprived of their dignity." Their stubbornness and unbelief was no excuse for heaping abuse upon them. "Despite the great obstinacy with which they continue to wage war against the gospel, we must not despise them, while we consider that, for the sake of the gospel, God's blessing still rests upon them. For the apostle indeed testifies that it will never be completely taken away: 'For the gifts and the calling of God are without repentance.'"[82]

The Evil of Antisemitism

Thomas Torrance made similar statements commenting specifically upon the Holocaust. "The Church today," he said, "cannot relate sincerely to Israel without acknowledging to the full the piled-up guilt of its rejection and persecution of Israel throughout the Christian centuries." We cannot merely point our finger of accusation against Hitler: "It cannot brush off the abominable horror of the mass extermination of Jews in modern times simply by putting it down to the Nazis." Modern antisemitism has "poisonous roots" going through many centuries of church history. We need to

79. Calvin, *Commentaries on the Epistle of Paul to the Romans*, 338.

80. Calvin, *Commentaries on the Epistle of Paul to the Romans*, 428.

81. Calvin, *Commentaries on the Epistle of Paul to the Romans*, 435.

82. Calvin, *Institutes of the Christian Religion*, vol. 2, 1336–37.

come to terms with the dark side of our history, which "discloses a deep-seated enmity that must constantly be dug out and submitted to the flame of divine judgment in the Cross of Jesus Christ."[83]

Hatred for the Jews, stated Torrance, is not a light matter: "He who attacks the Jews has to deal with God Almighty." The attitude of the heart is serious indeed: "He who harbours in his heart any spirit of anti-Semitism harbours in his heart the spirit of anti-Christ, for it all entails resentment against the Jew called Jesus." Far from despising the Jews, we should be like the "ten men" in the prophecy of Zechariah 8:23 from "all the languages of the nations" who "shall even take hold of the skirt of him that is a Jew, saying: We will go with you, for we have heard that God is with you." The skirt of the Jew, said Torrance, is to be found in the Old and New Testaments.[84] We are to "take hold of the mantle of the prophets" and "call upon the living God, the God of history, the God who has revealed Himself in the long story of Israel, the God who has come Himself in Jesus Christ." Destruction will come upon all who despise the Jews. Conversely, "he who returns to the Jew named Jesus, and finds in Him the incomparable Love of God, and very God of very God, even he will be saved."[85]

A Mainstream Reformed Doctrine

Calvin's belief that salvation would eventually come to Israel became the prevailing position in Reformed theology. Three English Puritans stand out in this connection. William Perkins (1558–1602) in his biblical commentary on Galatians 3:8, asserted, "In that the Lord says, 'All the nations shall be blessed in Abraham,' hence I gather that the nation of the Jews shall be called and converted to the participation of this blessing." We do not know the exact time and manner of this event: "When and how, God knows;

---

83. Torrance, "The Divine Vocation and Destiny of Israel in World History," 96.

84. Torrance, "Salvation Is of the Jews," 172.

85. Torrance, "Salvation Is of the Jews," 173.

but that it shall be done before the end of the world, we know."[86] Richard Sibbes (1577–1635) concurred with this perspective. Reflecting upon Noah's prophecy in Genesis 9:27 that God would enlarge Japheth and cause him to dwell in the tents of Shem, Sibbes affirmed, "The Jews are not yet come in under Christ's banner; but God, that hath persuaded Japhet to come into the tents of Shem, will persuade Shem to come into the tents of Japhet." The contemplation of the anticipated conversion of the Jews should bring happiness to the souls of Gentile believers: "The faithful Jews rejoiced to think of the calling of the Gentiles; and why should not we joy to think of the calling of the Jews?"[87]

John Owen stood in the same trajectory as Perkins and Sibbes. Romans 11 in his thinking was not the only biblical passage that taught the salvation of the Jews: "For although the promises under the Old Testament for the *calling of the Gentiles* were far more clear and numerous than those which remain concerning the *recalling of the Jews*, yet because the manner, way, and all the circumstances, were obscured, the whole is called a *mystery hid in God* from all the former ages of the church." Owen, like Calvin, believed that their recalling was an incomprehensible mystery. Owen wrote, "Who or what peculiar instruments he will use and employ for the final recovery of that miserable, lost people, whether he will do it by an ordinary or an extraordinary ministry, by gifts miraculous, or by the naked efficacy of the gospel, is known only in his own holy wisdom and counsel."[88]

The same perspective regarding the future salvation of Israel was found in Geneva in the seventeenth century. Francis Turretin (1623–1687) served as pastor of the Italian congregation and professor of theology at the Academy. There was no ambiguity in his declaration that "there will be a remarkable conversion of the Jews before the end of the world." There would be, he said, some mystery about their conversion: "As to the quality and extent of that conversion, whether it will be national and universal of all

---

86. Perkins, "Commentary on Galatians," 166.
87. Sibbes, "The Bruised Reed and Smoking Flax," 99.
88. Owen, *The Works of John Owen*, vol. 4, 440–41.

or particular of some; whether simultaneous or successive; and how, by what means and in what time it will go forward, is safer to be unknown than to be rashly defined." Turretin maintained that there is an application that follows from these considerations: "Thus we should labor in this most especially—that we may promote it not only by the preaching of sound doctrine, but also by the example of a better life, lest our conversation be a scandal to those obdurate Jews who for the most part estimate a doctrine from the life of its professors."[89]

Brakel, a contemporary of Turretin, ministered as a pastor in Rotterdam. He raised the question: "Will the Jewish nation always be a rejected nation, or will the entire nation yet come to repentance, believing and confessing that the Messiah has already come, and that Jesus is the Christ?" He answered in the affirmative. Brakel, unlike Turretin, did not hesitate to speak about a national conversion: "When speaking of the conversion of the Jews, we understand this to refer to the entire nation, and not only to Judah and Benjamin." "It also refers to the ten tribes."[90]

Brakel built his case in support of a future national conversion of Israel largely on the basis of detailed exegetical work in Romans 11. The beginning of his argumentation is illustrative of the direction that his exposition takes. Brakel drew attention to the question raised by Paul in verse 1: "I say then, hath God cast away His people?" "*God's people*," noted Brakel, is a reference to "the Jewish nation."[91] Paul answers his own question by way of "a negation and in a confirmation of the opposite." The negation in verse 1 "is stated with vehemence and indignation: 'God forbid.'" It would be "impossible" for "God" to "break His eternal covenant established with Abraham and his seed." The second part of Paul's response to the question raised is provided in verse 2: "God hath not cast away His people which He foreknew." "It is impossible," said Brakel, "that God would reject His people. They are His people and they will remain His people." "God has neither cast away His

---

89. Turretin, *Institutes of Elenctic Theology*, vol. 3, 587.
90. Brakel, *The Christian's Reasonable Service*, vol. 4, 510.
91. Brakel, *The Christian's Reasonable Service*, vol. 4, 511.

people *entirely*, nor will cast them away *ultimately*."[92] "The nation neither will nor can be cast away forever, but will come to repentance and be received again by God."[93]

Increase Mather and Jonathan Edwards in New England taught along the same lines as their Reformed predecessors.[94] Mather declared, "One of those great and glorious things which the world, especially, the people of God in the world, are in expectation of at this day, is *The general conversion of the* Israelitish *Nation*."[95] "Very many *Israelites* shall be saved." "In fact, not only a *Majority, but a very full and large Generality*."[96] Mather was delighted that more and more people were beginning to understand the biblical teaching on the future salvation of Israel: "The light of those truths which do concern the calling of the *Jews*, is wonderfully broken forth *of late time*." This marked a significant change: "Not long ago it seemed very paradoxical to affirm, that ever there should be a general conversion of the Jewish nation. But that truth of late hath gained ground much throughout the world."[97] The expectation of Scripture on the national conversion of the Jews had a practical application. "We should," wrote Mather, "pray for them, that they may see the salvation of the Lord."[98]

Jonathan Edwards (1703–1758) described the long history of Jewish unbelief and noted that instances "of the conversion of any of that nation have been so very rare since the destruction of Jerusalem."[99] He drew attention to the day when the prophecy of Zechariah 12:10 and its description of their contrition would be

92. Brakel, *The Christian's Reasonable Service*, vol. 4, 514.

93. Brakel, *The Christian's Reasonable Service*, vol. 4, 517.

94. Hesselink notes that Edwards believed that the Jews would return to their homeland and that the coming kingdom of Christ would be centered in the land of Israel. Hesselink, "The Millennium in the Reformed Tradition," 103.

95. Mather, *The Mystery of Israel's Salvation*, 2.

96. Mather, *The Mystery of Israel's Salvation*, 10.

97. Mather, *The Mystery of Israel's Salvation*, 44–45.

98. Mather, *The Mystery of Israel's Salvation*, 181.

99. Edwards, *A History of the Work of Redemption*, 381.

realized: "Divine grace shall melt and renew their hard hearts, 'and they shall look upon me whom they have pierced, and they shall mourn for him, as one mourneth for his only son.'" "The Jews," said Edwards, "shall flow to the blessed Jesus, penitently, humbly, and joyfully owning him as their glorious King and only Saviour." Like Owen, Edwards drew attention not only to Romans 11 and its teaching regarding the national conversion of the Jews, but also to the Hebrew Bible where the same prospect is held out: "There are also many passages of the Old Testament which cannot be interpreted in any other sense." Edwards expressed amazement that in divine providence the Jews have maintained their national identity for hundreds of years, even in their "dispersed condition." "The world," he said, "affords nothing else like it." The call of God to them will bring an amazing result: "That ancient people, who were alone God's people for so long a time," shall "be God's people again, never to be rejected more." The Jews and the Gentiles, as believers, will be gathered into one fold of God. But there will be one further development, affirmed Edwards. "So also shall the remains of the ten tribes, wherever they be, and though they have been rejected much longer than the Jews, be brought in with their brethren the Jews."[100]

Charles Hodge (1797–1878) at Princeton Theological Seminary appealed to the same biblical texts as did Edwards—Zechariah 12:10 and Romans 11—in his discussion concerning the restoration of the Jews to divine favor. He argued that two great events would precede the Second Coming of Christ, "the universal proclamation of the gospel" and the salvation of the Jews.[101] "The national conversion of the Jews" was not a sectarian belief on the theological fringe. It was a doctrinal position which was "according to the common faith of the Church."[102] Romans 11, he affirmed, teaches four main things: God had discarded the Jews for their rejection of Christ; the presence of a remnant according to the election of grace meant that there was not a universal casting

---

100. Edwards, *A History of the Work of Redemption*, 382.

101. Hodge, *Systematic Theology*, vol. 3, 800.

102. Hodge, *Systematic Theology*, vol. 3, 805.

off; the Jews were not cast off finally and decisively, but would be grafted in again after the fullness of the Gentiles had come in; and finally, according to Romans 11:26, all Israel will be saved. Hodge believed that there are two possible interpretations of this verse: "Whether this means the Jews as a nation, or the whole elect people of God including both Jews and Gentiles, may be doubtful." Either way, Romans 11 explicitly teaches "a national conversion of the Jews."[103]

John Murray (1898–1975) at Westminster Theological Seminary took the same view as Geerhardus Vos, his professor at Princeton Theological Seminary. Vos declared, "It seems to us that the conversion of Israel is clearly predicted." "Romans 11 speaks of a national conversion."[104] Murray, unlike Hodge, set forth a definitive position on Romans 11:26–27 and its statement that all Israel will be saved. Their future salvation, Paul states, would be in accordance with the prophetic announcement that the Deliverer would come from Zion turning away ungodliness from Jacob and that the Lord's covenant with them meant that he would take away their sins. Murray wrote, "It is of ethnic Israel Paul is speaking and Israel could not possibly include Gentiles."[105] The context, insisted Murray, demanded this understanding of Paul's statement: "If we keep in mind the theme of this chapter and the sustained emphasis on the restoration of Israel, there is no other alternative than to conclude that the proposition, 'all Israel shall be saved', is to be interpreted in terms of the fulness, the receiving, the ingrafting of Israel as a people, the restoration of Israel from unbelief to faith and repentance." The use of the word *all* did not necessarily mean that every last Israelite on the face of the earth would be converted: "The salvation of Israel must be conceived of on a scale that is commensurate with their trespass, their loss, their casting away, their breaking off, and their hardening, commensurate, of course,

---

103. Hodge, *Systematic Theology*, vol. 3, 807.
104. Vos, *Reformed Dogmatics*, 1123.
105. Murray, *The Epistle to the Romans*, 96.

in the opposite direction." The day will come, wrote Murray, when "the salvation of the mass of Israel" will come.[106]

Joel Beeke and Paul Smalley concur with the position of John Murray regarding the statement in Romans 11:26 that "all Israel shall be saved."[107] This is a reference, they argue, to "a spiritual awakening that will result in the salvation of a large number of the Jewish people alive at the time."[108] In support of this position, they appeal to the use of the phrase *pas Israel* in the Septuagint, which "appears dozens of times in the Greek Old Testament for Israel as a corporate people, though not every individual (Josh. 10:29–38; 2 Sam. 16:22; 1 Chron. 11:1 LXX)." In addition, the expression "all Israel" contrasts with the reference to "the remnant" in Romans 11:5. The "covenantal love" that God set upon Abraham and his descendants is the guarantee that "all Israel shall be saved."[109]

The Error of Replacement Theology

Thomas Torrance stood in continuity with the long tradition of Reformed teaching regarding the Jews and the unalterable call of God: "His wrath against Israel does not mean that he banishes Israel from his covenant of love and truth."[110] Reflecting the apostle's reasoning in Romans 11, Torrance noted that "the rejection of Israel worked out to the riches of the Gentiles." "They were blinded for us that we might see: they were stripped and deprived that we might become rich with the gospel." But this was not Paul's final point. There is more to his argument regarding the flow of redemptive history as he laid out the plan of God in Romans 11. There will be a restoration of Israel in terms of salvation coming to them in the last days. "Their restoration to life" will have "momentous

106. Murray, *The Epistle to the Romans*, 98.

107. Joel Beeke is Chancellor and Professor of Homiletics and Systematic Theology at Puritan Reformed Theological Seminary in Grand Rapids, Michigan. Paul Smalley is Research Assistant to the Chancellor.

108. Beeke and Smalley, *Reformed Systematic Theology*, vol. 4, 891.

109. Beeke and Smalley, *Reformed Systematic Theology*, vol. 4, 892.

110. Torrance, *Incarnation*, 54.

consequences." In fact, "the restoration of God's ancient people will have a part in the eschatological events of the consummation." "Even the full blessing of the Gentiles depends upon the fulfillment of the covenant promises to Israel." Torrance raised the question: "If the rejection of Israel brought reconciliation and riches of the world, what will the restoration of Israel involve but life from the dead?"[111]

Torrance further stressed that this doctrine of the irrevocable call of God to the Jews is not a secondary issue: "That God does not go back upon his distinctive covenant with Israel or change his mind about his special gifts to Israel or revoke his calling of Israel for universal mission, is central not only to the message of the Old Testament but to the message of the New Testament as well."[112] Paul's declaration in Romans 11:29 that the gifts and the calling of God are irrevocable underscores the mistake of replacement theology. Torrance affirmed that "the Roman Church gave currency to the false idea that Israel was the People of God only according the flesh and had to be replaced by the Church of Jesus Christ as the People of God according to the Spirit."[113]

Torrance recognized the crucial significance of Romans 11:17–18 in the question of whether or not Israel has been replaced as the people of God. Paul in this passage identifies Gentile believers as being wild olive shoots that have been grafted into the cultivated olive tree, namely Israel. He admonishes them not to be arrogant and reminds them that they do not support the root, but the root supports them.[114] Torrance commented, "If in their rejection of Jesus as the Messiah Jews appear to have broken themselves off as natural branches from the trunk of Israel, and Gentiles like

111. Torrance, *Incarnation*, 55.

112. Torrance, "The Divine Vocation and Destiny of Israel in World History," 85.

113. Torrance, "The Divine Vocation and Destiny of Israel in World History," 92.

114. Torrance and Taylor advanced the position that "in her sin the Church is proud." Specifically, "in her pride she has frequently, from early times, claimed that the Church has replaced Israel as the chosen people of God." Torrance and Taylor, *Israel, God's Servant*, 6.

wild olive branches are grafted on to it, the trunk which gives all the branches their life remains." What conclusion must be drawn? Said Torrance, "Thus the covenanted people of God as such is not discarded with the foundation and expansion of the Christian Church." The entire argument in Romans 11 instructs us in the truth of the unsearchable judgments and inscrutable ways of God: "What happened to the Jews, when, through their blindness, they rejected their Messiah, took place for our sake, that we Gentiles might through them be reconciled to God, but our reconciliation will not be fulfilled apart from the reconciliation of Israel also."[115]

The Future of Israel

Torrance in these statements was articulating the same perspectives as those of Robert Murray M'Cheyne who affirmed that "the race of Israel" has been "preserved for some great purpose in the world."[116] Reflecting his own determination to "keep up a knowledge of the prophecies regarding Israel," M'Cheyne drew attention to a significant prophetic statement in Zechariah 8.[117] Verse 8 indicated, he said, that "the time is coming when they shall be as great a blessing as they have been a curse. Specifically, there is the statement in verse 23 that the days would come when ten men from the nations shall grasp the sleeve of a Jew, asking that they might go with him because they had heard that God was with them.[118] M'Cheyne declared, "This has never been fulfilled; but as the word of God is true, this is true." Indeed, "the Jews are to be the great missionaries of the world."[119]

115. Torrance, "The Divine Vocation and Destiny of Israel in World History," 91.

116. Bonar, *Robert Murray M'Cheyne*, 495.

117. Bonar, *Robert Murray M'Cheyne*, 87–88.

118. Bonar, *Robert Murray M'Cheyne*, 495.

119. Bonar, *Robert Murray M'Cheyne*, 496.

Conclusion

CALVIN DEDICATED HIS ENTIRE life to the study and teaching of the Bible, which in his view was not merely a human production.[1] Calvin exhorted, "Whoever then wishes to profit in the Scriptures, let him, first of all, lay down this as a settled point, that the Law and the Prophets are not a doctrine delivered according to the will and pleasure of men, but dictated by the Holy Spirit."[2] Scripture, he maintained, was "the oracle and eternal truth of the Highest King, Lord of heaven, earth, and the sea, and King of Kings." Its nature as divine revelation had enormous implications. It was to be "received with the highest reverence by all peoples, times, and classes."[3] In fact, "we owe to the Scripture the same reverence which we owe to God; because it has proceeded from him alone."[4]

Scripture, as the Word of God, had to be handled by expositors with great care. Said Calvin, "He surely cannot be endured, who, with impure, or even with unprepared hands, will handle that very thing, which of all things is the most sacred on earth."[5] The responsibility of the preacher and "expounder" was straightforward: "It is almost his only work to lay open the mind of the writer

1. Calvin sharply contrasts with Walter Brueggemann on the production of the Old Testament. Brueggemann, *Chosen? Reading the Bible amid the Israeli-Palestinian Conflict*, 2.

2. Calvin, *Commentaries on the Second Epistle to Timothy*, 249.

3. Calvin, "John Calvin's Latin Preface to Olivétan's French Bible," 374.

4. Calvin, *Commentaries on the Second Epistle to Timothy*, 249.

5. Calvin, *Commentary on the Epistle of Paul to the Romans*, xxvii.

whom he undertakes to explain."[6] His announced commitment in this connection was to a vigorous rejection of allegorical exegesis in favor of a literal hermeneutic: "The true meaning of Scripture is the natural and obvious meaning." "Let us," furthermore, "boldly set aside as deadly corruptions, those pretended expositions, which lead us away from the natural meaning."[7]

It was this hermeneutical commitment which led him to maintain on the basis of his exegetical work in the Scripture that the Lord loved Abraham and his offspring unto a thousand generations. He set his heart upon them and chose them to be his children forever, even though many were broken off from the covenant community as a result of their unbelief. They continued to be in the view of Calvin and mainstream Reformed theology a special nation loved by God who in the time of the divine appointment would experience national conversion and salvation.

Although Calvin ever holds a place of honor and even preeminence within the Reformed community, there are biblical scholars within that broad theological tradition who have dissented from him in terms of his hermeneutical approach when it comes to the Old Testament prophets. John MacArthur, for example, states, "Calvin proved to be *inconsistent* in the application of his own commitment to literal hermeneutics, especially when he came to end-times prophecy." He adds, "In millennial passages, the Reformer all-too-quickly jettisoned his own literal hermeneutic and used an allegorical approach instead."[8] This is an interesting observation. Did Calvin in his rejection of allegorical exegesis ever resort to it in his handling of the prophets?[9]

---

6. Calvin, *Commentary on the Epistle of Paul to the Romans*, xxiii.

7. Calvin, *Commentaries on the Epistle of Paul to the Galatians*, 136.

8. MacArthur, "Does Calvinism Lead to Futuristic Premillennialism?", 144.

9. G. Sujin Pak affirms that Calvin "rejected allegorical readings in favor of *figural* and *metaphorical* readings" of Old Testament passages. He attempted "to differentiate the proper practices of figural reading over and against improper allegorical exegesis." Pak, "Calvin beyond Literal and Allegorical Reading," 25.

A Metaphorical Reading of the Prophets

Calvin did use the term *allegorical* in a positive way on at least one occasion, even though he warned against the allegorical approach of the Alexandrian school of interpretation in the strongest terms: "We must, however, entirely reject the allegories of Origen, and others like him, which Satan, with the deepest subtlety, has endeavoured to introduce into the Church, for the purpose of rendering the doctrine of Scripture ambiguous and destitute of all certainty and firmness."[10] He even warned about applying allegorical exegesis to Old Testament prophetic passages like Zechariah 6:1 with its reference to a chariot with red horses, a second one with black horses, a third one with white horses, and a fourth one with dappled horses. Calvin commented, "But as the vision is obscure, interpreters have given it different meanings." He cited one proposal which he regarded as being remote from the true sense: "They who think that the four Gospels are designated by the four chariots, give a very frigid view." He then gave a warning: "I have elsewhere reminded you, that we are to avoid these futile refinements which of themselves vanish away. Allegories, I know, delight many; but we ought reverently and soberly to interpret the prophetic writings, and not to fly in the clouds, but ever to fix our foot on solid ground."[11] Calvin asserted here that our handling of prophecy must be undertaken on the solid ground of a literal hermeneutic. Did Calvin consistently apply his literal hermeneutic in his interpretation of Old Testament prophetic passages?

Let us consider the exegetical approach of Calvin and compare it with that of John MacArthur who positions himself within the Reformed theological tradition.[12] MacArthur maintains that Isaiah 30:18–26 is a presentation of the future Millennium. The description of the spiritual blessings that will come to Israel are

10. Calvin, *Commentaries on the Book of Genesis*, vol. 1, 114.

11. Calvin, *Commentaries on the Prophet Zechariah*, 140.

12. MacArthur contends that Reformed theology is rooted in the Bible. MacArthur, "Does Calvinism Lead to Futuristic Premillennialism?", 141–42. In his volume on systematic theology he refers to Calvin as "the great Reformer." MacArthur and Mayhue, *Biblical Doctrine*, 623.

clearly stated: "O people in Zion, inhabitants in Jerusalem, you will weep no longer. He will surely be gracious to you at the sound of your cry; when he hears it, he will answer you" (vs. 19). There then follows a remarkable statement regarding the presence of the Lord among his people Israel: "Although the Lord has given you bread of privation and water of oppression, he, your Teacher will no longer hide himself, but your eyes will behold your Teacher. And your ears will hear a word behind you, 'This the way, walk in it,' whenever you turn to the right or to the left" (vss. 20–21). Physical and material promises then follow in the passage: "Then he will give you rain for the seed which you will sow in the ground, and bread from the yield of the ground, and it will be rich and plenteous; on that day your livestock will graze in a roomy pasture. Also the oxen and the donkeys which work the ground will eat salted fodder, which has been winnowed with shovel and fork. On every lofty mountain and on every high hill there will be streams running with water on the day of the great slaughter, when the towers fall" (vss. 23–25).[13] MacArthur with his commitment to a consistently literal hermeneutic comments, "In the messianic kingdom of that future day, agriculture, cattle raising, food production, and water resources will prosper."[14]

How did Calvin interpret the same passage? One might expect that he would have taken a similar approach to the text as that taken by MacArthur. Calvin, after all, did insist that "the true meaning of Scripture is the natural and obvious meaning." He further exhorted his readers, "Let us embrace and abide by it resolutely."[15] Calvin, though, argued against a literal interpretation in favor of a figurative understanding of the prophet's statements regarding agricultural prosperity and abundant water resources.[16] "When the prophets describe the kingdom of Christ,"

13. This quotation from Isaiah 30 is from the New American Standard Bible.

14. MacArthur, *The MacArthur Study Bible*, 1446.

15. Calvin, *Commentaries on the Epistle of Paul to the Galatians*, 136.

16. We find the same kind of approach with Isaiah 2:3 in which the prophet announces the streaming of the nations to Zion. De Greef summarizes

he said, "they commonly draw metaphors from the ordinary life of men." MacArthur in his advocacy of a consistent literalism would have no problem with recognizing the presence of metaphorical language in Scripture, but Calvin went one step further in his commentary on the material blessings prophesied in the passage for Israel dwelling in their land: "Those expressions are allegorical, and are accommodated by the Prophet to our ignorance, that we may know, by means of those things which are perceived by our senses, those blessings which have so great and surpassing excellence that our minds cannot comprehend them."[17]

The Everlasting Possession of the Land

Those who are committed to a consistently plain and natural reading of the biblical text within the Reformed community would note that Calvin's heavy reliance upon metaphor and allegory in the Isaiah passage is not an isolated instance of a departure from a literal hermeneutic. The same thing is found in his biblical commentary on Amos 9:13–15, a text which prophecies agricultural prosperity following a return of Israel from exile to their land and the promise that they would reside there never to be uprooted from it again. The land, Amos states, will be incredibly fertile. Farmers will want to plant seed for the next harvest, but they will be slowed down by the reapers who will still be gathering up the harvest from the previous year.[18] The mountains will be dripping with sweet wine, and all the hills shall be flowing with it. God himself will be the one to bring Israel back to the land. They will rebuild their cities and live in them. They will plant vineyards and make gardens, drinking and eating the produce thereof. The prophecy concludes with a culminating statement. The Lord announces in the most explicit

how Calvin handled the passage: "Going to Zion, where the temple was located and sacrifices were offered" is a "figurative mode of expression and a way of emphasizing a relationship with God." De Greef, *Of One Tree*, 87.

17. Calvin, *Commentary on the Book of the Prophet Isaiah*, vol. 2, 375.

18. Jelinek, "Amos," 1356.

terms possible: "I will plant them in their land, and no longer shall they be pulled up from the land I have given them" (vs. 15).

John Jelinek embraces a straightforward literal approach to the text asserting that "nothing in Israel's historical restoration after exile fulfilled the promises given here" and maintaining that "in the Messiah's kingdom" the "curse that afflicts creation" is "lifted and the productivity of the land returns." "Israel," he says, "will put roots down in the promised land, never to leave it again."[19] Mac-Arthur sees this as "the ultimate fulfillment of God's land promise to Abraham."[20] The promise given to Abraham of the land had referred to the permanent possession of it. Genesis 13:15 had stated, "All the land which you see I give to you and your descendants forever." And Genesis 17:8 had added, "I give to you and your descendants after you the land in which you are a stranger, all the land of Canaan, as an everlasting possession; and I will be their God."

Calvin, though, moved away from a literal understanding of the passage in favor of figures of speech, specifically metaphors, and even recognized that some of his readers would have problems with his flirtation with allegory. Said Calvin, "Whenever the Prophets set forth promises of a happy and prosperous state to God's people, they adopt metaphorical expressions, and say, that abundance of all good things shall flow, that there shall be the most fruitful produce, that provisions shall be bountifully supplied; for they accommodated their mode of speaking to the notions of that ancient people." The point, argued Calvin, is that "the Spirit under these figurative expressions declares, that the kingdom of Christ shall in every way be happy and blessed, or that the Church of God, which means the same thing, shall be blessed, when Christ shall begin to reign."[21] "What is here said of the abundance of corn and wine," he said, "must be explained with reference to the nature of Christ's kingdom. As then the kingdom of Christ is spiritual, it is enough for us, that it abounds in spiritual blessings."[22] As to the

19. Jelinek, "Amos," 1356.
20. MacArthur, *The MacArthur Study Bible*, 1870.
21. Calvin, *Commentaries on the Prophet* Amos, 410.
22. Calvin, *Commentaries on the Prophet* Amos, 413.

Lord's declaration that he would plant them permanently in the land, never to be uprooted again, Calvin appears to have toned down the meaning, not articulating any idea of "an unconditional promise of permanent possession" on the part of Israel.[23] He merely stated, "The Prophet says, that the people, when restored, would be in a state of tranquility."[24]

Calvin was aware that certain of his readers would be happier with a more literal understanding of the final paragraph of the prophecy of Amos and therefore offered a defense of his exposition of the passage: "If any one objects and says, that the Prophet does not speak here allegorically; the answer is ready at hand, even this,—that it is a manner of speaking everywhere found in Scripture, that a happy state is painted as it were before our eyes by setting before us the conveniences of the present life and earthly blessings." "The Prophets," he affirmed, "accommodated their style" to "the capacities of a rude and weak people."[25]

Diversity in the Reformed Tradition

This study reminds us that Reformed theology from the time of Calvin up through the teaching of Thomas Torrance has not produced a monolithic doctrine with respect to the Jews and the prospect of a future restoration of the Davidic kingdom centered in Jerusalem with Christ ruling over the nations in a literal millennium.[26] Calvin rejected such a prospect while other theologians in continuity with early church fathers advocated the position. The different points of view are due to the issue of hermeneutics and the degree to which a particular exegete was committed to a consistently literal reading of prophetic passages or recognized the legitimacy of a metaphorical reading of the same.

23. Schultz, "Amos," 132.

24. Calvin, *Commentaries on the Prophet* Amos, 412.

25. Calvin, *Commentaries on the Prophet* Amos, 413.

26. "The Reformed tradition," notes Richard Muller, is "a highly diverse tradition." Muller, "Diversity in the Reformed Tradition," 12.

We ever need to be realistic with respect to the outcome of biblical interpretation. Calvin stated, "What would otherwise be very desirable cannot be expected in this life, that is, universal consent among us in the interpretation of all parts of Scripture." "Even those who have not been deficient in their zeal for piety, nor in reverence and sobriety in handling the mysteries of God, have by no means agreed among themselves on every point; for God hath never favoured his servants with so great a benefit, that they were all endued with a full and perfect knowledge in every thing." Calvin further stated that we should not bemoan the lack of perfect concord when it comes to the results of our biblical exegesis. There are at least two advantages resulting from different perspectives regarding the meaning of the biblical text. The lack of full agreement is "no doubt," said Calvin, "for this end—that he might first keep them humble; and secondly, render them disposed to cultivate brotherly intercourse."[27]

There has not been perfect unanimity among the biblical scholars whom we have considered regarding the meaning of certain passages in the Holy Scripture. Nevertheless, as we have seen, mainstream Reformed doctrine has ever maintained that the Jews are a people who have been chosen and loved by God and have been promised salvation through faith in Christ. Although they have been temporarily set aside due to their unbelief, this will not last forever: "Blindness in part has happened to Israel until the fullness of the Gentiles has come in" (Rom 11:25). The day will then come when God "will pour on the house of David and on the inhabitants of Jerusalem the Spirit of grace and supplication." "Then they will look on Me," says the Lord, "whom they pierced." Deep contrition will follow: "Yes, they will mourn for Him as one mourns for his only son, and grieve for Him as one grieves for a firstborn" (Zech 12:10). They will experience moral cleansing: "In that day a fountain shall be opened for the house of David and for the inhabitants of Jerusalem, for sin and for uncleanness" (Zech 13:1). "And so all Israel will be saved" (Rom 11:26).

---

27. Calvin, *Commentary on the Epistle of Paul to the Romans*, xxvii.

Selected Bibliography

Armstrong, Brian G. "Exegetical and Theological Principles in Calvin's Preaching, with Special Attention to His Sermons on the Psalms." In *Ordenlich und Fruchtbar*, edited by Wilhelm H. Neuser et al., 191–209. Leiden: J. J. Groen en Zoon, 1997.

———. "The Nature and Structure of Calvin's Thought according to the *Institutes*: Another Look." In *John Calvin's Institutes: His Opus Magnum*, 55–81. Potchefstroom: Potchefstroom University for Christian Higher Education, 1986.

Augustine. *Concerning the City of God against the Pagans*. Translated by Henry Bettenson. London: Penguin, 1984.

Austin, Kenneth. *From Judaism to Calvinism: The Life and Writings of Immanuel Tremellius*. Aldershot, UK: Ashgate, 2007.

———. *The Jews and the Reformation*. New Haven: Yale University Press, 2020.

Balserak, Jon. *Establishing the Remnant Church in France: Calvin's Lectures on the Minor Prophets, 1556–1559*. Leiden: Brill, 2011.

———. *John Calvin as Sixteenth-Century Prophet*. Oxford: Oxford University Press, 2014.

Baron, Salo W. "John Calvin and the Jews." In *Essential Papers on Judaism and Christianity in Conflict*, edited by Jeremy Cohen, 380–400. New York: NYU Press, 1991.

Barth, Karl. *Church Dogmatics*, vol. 4, part 1. Translated by G. W. Bromiley. London: T&T Clark, 2004.

———. *Church Dogmatics*, vol. 4, part 2. Translated by G. W. Bromiley. London: T&T Clark, 2004.

———. *Church Dogmatics*, vol. 4, part 3.3. Translated by G. W. Bromiley. London: T&T Clark, 2004.

Bavinck, Herman. *Reformed Dogmatics*, vol. 3. Translated by John Vriend. Grand Rapids: Baker, 2006.

Beeke, Joel R. "Calvin on Piety." In *The Cambridge Companion to John Calvin*, edited by Donald K. McKim, 125–52. Cambridge: Cambridge University Press, 2004.

Beeke, Joel R., and Paul M. Smalley. *Reformed Systematic Theology*, vol. 4. Wheaton, IL: Crossway, 2024.

Benedict, Philip. *Christ's Churches Purely Reformed: A Social History of Calvinism*. New Haven: Yale University Press, 2002.

Beza, Theodore. *The Life of John Calvin*. Translated by Henry Beveridge. Philadelphia: Westminster, 1909.

Blacketer, Raymond A. "Calvin as Commentator on the Mosaic Harmony and Joshua." In *Calvin and the Bible*, edited by Donald K. McKim, 30–52. Cambridge: Cambridge University Press, 2006.

Boice, James Montgomery. *Foundations of the Christian Faith*. Downers Grove, IL: InterVarsity, 1986

———. *The Last and Future World*. Grand Rapids: Zondervan, 1974.

Bonar, Andrew A. *Robert Murray M'Cheyne: Memoir and Remains*. London: Banner of Truth, 1966.

Bouwsma, William J. *John Calvin: A Sixteenth-Century Portrait*. New York: Oxford University Press, 1988.

Brakel, Wilhelmus à. *The Christian's Reasonable Service*, vol. 4. Translated by Bartel Elshout. Grand Rapids: Reformation Heritage, 1995.

Brueggemann, Walter. *Chosen? Reading the Bible amid the Israeli-Palestinian Conflict*. Louisville: Westminster John Knox, 2015.

Bullinger, Heinrich. "A Brief Exposition of the One and Eternal Testament or Covenant of God." In Charles S. McCoy and J. Wayne Baker, *Fountainhead of Federalism: Heinrich Bullinger and the Covenant Tradition*, 99–138. Translated by Charles S. McCoy and J. Wayne Baker. Louisville: Westminster John Knox, 1991.

———. "The Second Helvetic Confession." In *The Creeds of Christendom*, vol. 3, edited by Philip Schaff, 831–909. Grand Rapids: Baker, 1990.

Burge, Gary. *Jesus and the Land: The New Testament Challenge to "Holy Land" Theology*. Grand Rapids: Baker, 2010.

Calvin, John. *Commentaries on the Book of Genesis*. Calvin's Commentaries, vols. 1–2. Translated by John King. Grand Rapids: Baker, 1979.

———. *Commentaries on the Book of Joshua*. Calvin's Commentaries. Translated by Henry Beveridge. Grand Rapids: Baker, 1979.

———. *Commentaries on the Book of the Prophet Daniel*. Calvin's Commentaries, vols. 1–2. Translated by Thomas Myers. Grand Rapids: Baker, 1979.

———. *Commentaries on the Epistle of Paul to the Ephesians*. Calvin's Commentaries. Translated by William Pringle. Grand Rapids: Baker, 1979.

———. *Commentaries on the Epistle of Paul to the Galatians*. Calvin's Commentaries. Translated by William Pringle. Grand Rapids: Baker, 1979.

———. *Commentaries on the Epistle of Paul to the Hebrews*. Calvin's Commentaries. Translated by John Owen. Grand Rapids: Baker, 1979.

———. *Commentaries on the Epistle of Paul the Apostle to the Romans*. Calvin's Commentaries. Translated by John Owen. Grand Rapids: Baker, 1979.

———. *Commentaries on the First Epistle of Peter*. Calvin's Commentaries. Translated by John Owen. Grand Rapids: Baker, 1979.

———. *Commentaries on the Last Four Books of Moses Arranged in the Form of a Harmony.* Calvin's Commentaries, vols. 1–4. Translated by Charles William Bingham. Grand Rapids: Baker, 1979.

———. *Commentaries on the Prophet Amos.* Calvin's Commentaries. Translated by John Owen. Grand Rapids: Baker, 1979.

———. *Commentaries on the Prophet Ezekiel.* Calvin's Commentaries, vols. 1–2. Translated by Thomas Myers. Grand Rapids: Baker, 1979.

———. *Commentaries on the Prophet Habakkuk.* Calvin's Commentaries. Translated by John Owen. Grand Rapids: Baker, 1979.

———. *Commentaries on the Prophet Hosea.* Calvin's Commentaries. Translated by John Owen. Grand Rapids: Baker, 1979.

———. *Commentaries on the Prophet Jeremiah and the Lamentations.* Calvin's Commentaries, vols. 1–5. Translated by John Owen. Grand Rapids: Baker, 1979.

———. *Commentaries on the Prophet Micah.* Calvin's Commentaries. Translated by John Owen. Grand Rapids: Baker, 1979.

———. *Commentaries on the Prophet Zechariah.* Calvin's Commentaries. Translated by John Owen. Grand Rapids: Baker, 1979.

———. *Commentaries on the Second Epistle to Timothy.* Calvin's Commentaries. Translated by William Pringle. Grand Rapids: Baker, 1979.

———. *Commentary on a Harmony of the Evangelists.* Calvin's Commentaries, vols. 1–4. Translated by William Pringle. Grand Rapids: Baker, 1979.

———. *Commentary on the Book of the Prophet Isaiah.* Calvin's Commentaries, vols. 1–4. Translated by William Pringle. Grand Rapids: Baker, 1979.

———. *Commentary on the Book of Psalms.* Calvin's Commentaries, vols. 1–5. Translated by James Anderson. Grand Rapids: Baker, 1979.

———. *Commentary on the First Epistle of Paul to the Corinthians.* Calvin's Commentaries. Translated by John Pringle. Grand Rapids: Baker, 1979.

———. *Commentary on the Gospel according to John.* Calvin's Commentaries, vol. 1. Translated by William Pringle Grand Rapids: Baker, 1979.

———. *Commentary on the Second Epistle of Paul to the Corinthians.* Calvin's Commentaries. Translated by John Pringle. Grand Rapids: Baker, 1979.

———. *Commentary upon the Acts of the Apostles.* Calvin's Commentaries, vols. 1–2. Translated by Henry Beveridge. Grand Rapids: Baker, 1979.

———. *Institutes of the Christian Religion.* 1541 Edition. Translated by Robert White. Edinburgh: Banner of Truth, 2014.

———. *Institutes of the Christian Religion*, vols. 1–2. Translated by Ford Lewis Battles. Philadelphia: Westminster, 1960.

———. "John Calvin's Latin Preface to Olivétan's French Bible." In John Calvin, *Institutes of the Christian Religion*, 373–77. Translated by Ford Lewis Battles. Grand Rapids: Eerdmans, 1986.

———. *Sermons on Genesis: Chapters 11–20.* Translated by Rob Roy McGregor. Edinburgh: Banner of Truth, 2012.

———. *Sermons on 2 Samuel: Chapters 1–13.* Translated by Douglas Kelly. Edinburgh: Banner of Truth, 1992.

————. *Sermons on Titus*. Translated by Robert White. Edinburgh: Banner of Truth, 2015.

Campi, Emidio. "Calvin, the Swiss Reformed Churches, and the European Reformation." In *Calvin and His Influence, 1509–2009*, edited by Irena Backus et al., 119–43. Oxford: Oxford University Press, 2011.

Chafer, Lewis Sperry. *Systematic Theology*, vol. 4. Grand Rapids: Kregel, 1976.

Chapman, Colin. *Christian Zionism and the Restoration of Israel: How Should We Interpret the Scriptures?* Eugene, OR: Cascade, 2021.

Chrysostom, John. "Homilies on the Gospel of Saint Matthew" In *Nicene and Post-Nicene Fathers*, vol. 10, edited by Philip Schaff, 456–62. Edinburgh: T & T Clark; Grand Rapids: Eerdmans, 1991.

Coffey, John. *Exodus and Liberation: Deliverance Politics from John Calvin to Martin Luther King Jr.* Oxford: Oxford University Press, 2014.

Cooper, Henry R. "Christian Hebraism in the Renaissance and Reformation: Croatia?" *Colloquia Maruliana* 23 (2014) 185–96.

Cottret, Bernard. *Calvin: A Biography*. Translated by M. Wallace McDonald. Grand Rapids: Eerdmans, 2000.

De Greef, Wulfert. "Calvin As Commentator on the Psalms." In *Calvin and the Bible*, edited by Donald K. McKim, 85–106. Cambridge: Cambridge University Press, 2006.

————. *Of One Tree: Calvin on Jews and Christians in the Context of the Late Middle Ages*. Translated by Lyle D. Bierma. Göttingen: Vandenhoeck & Ruprecht, 2021.

Detmers, Achim. "Calvin, the Jews, and Judaism." In *Jews, Judaism, and the Reformation in Sixteenth-Century Germany*, edited by Dean Phillip Bell et al., 197–217. Leiden: Brill, 2006.

DeVries, Dawn. "Calvin's Preaching." In *The Cambridge Companion to John Calvin*, edited by Donald K. McKim, 106–24. Cambridge: Cambridge University Press, 2004.

Donnelly, John Patrick. "Italian Influences on the Development of Calvinist Scholasticism." *Sixteenth Century Journal* 7 (1976) 81–101.

Edwards, Jonathan. *A History of the Work of Redemption*. Edinburgh: Banner of Truth, 2003.

Engammare, Max. "Calvin the Workaholic." In *Calvin and His Influence, 1509–2009*, edited by Irena Backus et al., 67–83. Oxford: Oxford University Press, 2011.

Fesko, J. V. *Beyond Calvin: Union with Christ and Justification in Early Modern Reformed Theology (1517–1700)*. Göttingen: Vandenhoeck & Ruprecht, 2012.

Frame, John M. *Systematic Theology: An Introduction to Christian Belief*. Phillipsburg, NJ: Presbyterian and Reformed, 2013.

Gamble, Richard C. *The Whole Counsel of God*, vol. 1. Phillipsburg, NJ: Presbyterian and Reformed, 2009.

Ganoczy, Alexandre. "Calvin, John." In *The Oxford Encyclopedia of the Reformation*, edited by Hans J. Hillerbrand, 234–39. New York: Oxford University Press, 1996.

————. "Calvin's Life." In *The Cambridge Companion to John Calvin*, edited by Donald K. McKim, 3–24. Cambridge: Cambridge University Press, 2004.

Gordon, Bruce. *Calvin*. New Haven: Yale University Press, 2009.

————. *Zwingli: God's Armed Prophet*. New Haven: Yale University Press, 2021.

Greef, Wulfert de. "Calvin as Commentator on the Psalms." In *Calvin and the Bible*, edited by Donald K. McKim, 85–106. Cambridge: Cambridge University Press, 2006.

————. *The Writings of John Calvin: An Introductory Guide*. Grand Rapids: Baker, 1993.

Gritsch, Eric W. "The Jews in Reformation Theology." In *Jewish-Christian Encounters over the Centuries: Symbiosis, Prejudice, Holocaust, Dialogue*, edited by Marvin Perry et al., 197–213. New York: Peter Lang, 1994.

Hannah, John D. *An Uncommon Union: Dallas Theological Seminary and American Evangelicalism*. Grand Rapids: Zondervan, 2009.

Hart, Darryl G. *Calvinism: A History*. New Haven: Yale University Press, 2013.

Hesselink, I. John. "Calvin on the Relation of the Church and Israel Based Largely on His Interpretation of Romans 9–11." In *Calvin As Exegete*, edited by Peter De Klerk, 95–110. Calvin Studies Society, 1993.

————. "The Millennium in the Reformed Tradition." *Reformed Review* 52, no. 2 (Winter 1998–1999) 97–125.

Hill, Christopher. "The Conversion of the Jews." In *Millenarianism and Messianism in English Literature and Thought*, edited by Richard H. Popkin, 12–36. Leiden: Brill, 1988.

Hobbs, R. Gerald. "Bucer, the Jews, and Judaism." In *Jews, Judaism, and the Reformation in Sixteenth-Century Germany*, edited by Dean Phillip Bell et al., 137–69. Leiden: Brill, 2006.

Hodge, Charles. *Systematic Theology*, vol. 3. Grand Rapids: Eerdmans, 1975.

Holwerda, David E. "Eschatology and History: A Look at Calvin's Eschatological Vision." In *Exploring the Heritage of John Calvin*, edited by David E. Holwerda, 110–39. Grand Rapids: Baker, 1976.

Horton, Michael S. *The Christian Faith: A Systematic Theology for Pilgrims on the Way*. Grand Rapids: Zondervan, 2011.

————. "Covenant Theology." In *Covenantal and Dispensational Theologies: Four Views on the Continuity of Scripture*, edited by Brent E. Parker et al., 35–73. Downers Grove, IL: InterVarsity, 2022.

Huijgen, Arnold. "Calvin's Old Testament Theology and Beyond: Paradoxes, Problems, and Comparisons with the Approaches of Arnold van Ruler and Kornelis Heiko Miskotte." In *The Oxford Handbook of Calvin and Calvinism*, edited by Bruce Gordon et al., 88–104. Oxford: Oxford University Press, 2021.

Hunsinger, George. "Thomas F. Torrance: A Eulogy." *Participatio: Journal of the Thomas F. Torrance Theological Fellowship* 1 (2009) 11–12.

Irenaeus. "Against Heresies." In *The Ante-Nicene Fathers*, vol. 1, edited by Alexander Roberts et al, 309–567. Edinburgh: T&T Clark; Grand Rapids: Eerdmans, 1996.

Jelinek, John A. "Amos." In *The Moody Bible Commentary*, edited by Michael Rydelnik et al., 1341–56. Chicago: Moody, 2014.

Jue, Jeffrey K. "A Millennial Genealogy: Joseph Mede, Jonathan Edwards, and Old Princeton." In *Resurrection and Eschatology: Theology in Service of the Church*, edited by Lane G. Tipton et al., 396–423. Phillipsburg, NJ: Presbyterian and Reformed, 2008.

———. "Puritan Millenarianism in Old and New England." In *The Cambridge Companion to Puritanism*, edited by John Coffey et al., 259–76. Cambridge: Cambridge University Press, 2008.

Justin Martyr. "Dialogue with Trypho, a Jew." In *The Ante-Nicene Fathers*, vol. 1, edited by Alexander Roberts et al., 194–270. Edinburgh: T&T Clark, 1996.

Kammerling, Joy. "Andreas Osiander's Sermons on the Jews." *Lutheran Quarterly* 15 (2001) 59–84.

———. "Andreas Osiander, the Jews, and Judaism." In *Jews, Judaism, and the Reformation in Sixteenth-Century Germany*, edited by Dean Phillip Bell et al., 219–47. Leiden: Brill, 2006.

Kelly, Douglas F. *Systematic Theology: Grounded in Holy Scripture and Understood in the Light of the Church*, vol. 1. Fearn, UK: Mentor, 2008.

———. *Systematic Theology: Grounded in Holy Scripture and Understood in the Light of the Church*, vol. 3. Fearn, UK: Mentor, 2021.

Kirn, Hans-Martin. "Ulrich Zwingli, the Jews, and Judaism." In *Jews, Judaism, and the Reformation in Sixteenth-Century Germany*, edited by Dean Phillip Bell et al., 171–95. Leiden: Brill, 2006.

Keil, Carl Friedrich, and Franz Delitzsch. *The Pentateuch*. Translated by James Martin. Grand Rapids: Eerdmans, 1976.

Klempa, William. "The First-Born in God's Family." In *Calvin@500: Theology, History, and Practice*, edited by Richard R. Topping et al., 1–22. Eugene, OR: Pickwick, 2011.

Kooi, Christine. "Who Were the Israelites in the Netherlandish Reformation?" In *The Old Testament, Calvin and the Reformed Tradition*, edited by Yudha Thianto, 111–32. Leiden: Brill, 2024.

Letham, Robert. *Systematic Theology*. Wheaton, IL: Crossway, 2019.

MacArthur, John. "Does Calvinism Lead to Futuristic Premillennialism?" In *Christ's Prophetic Plans: A Futuristic Premillennial Primer*, edited by John MacArthur et al., 141–59. Chicago: Moody, 2012.

———. *The MacArthur Study Bible*. Nashville, TN: Thomas Nelson, 1982.

MacArthur, John, and Richard Mayhue. *Biblical Doctrine: A Systematic Summary of Bible Truth*. Wheaton, IL: Crossway, 2017.

MacCulloch, Diarmaid. "Calvin: Fifth Latin Doctor of the Church?" In *Calvin and His Influence, 1509–2009*, edited by Irena Backus et al., 33–45. Oxford: Oxford University Press, 2011.

Manetsch, Scott. "Jeremiah in Geneva: Pastoral Theology in John Calvin's Lectures on the Book of the Prophet Jeremiah." In *The Old Testament, Calvin and the Reformed Tradition*, edited by Yudha Thianto, 33–57. Leiden: Brill, 2024.

Mather, Cotton. *Biblia Americana: Genesis*, edited by Reiner Smolinski. Grand Rapids: Baker, 2010.

Mather, Increase. *The Mystery of Israel's Salvation Explained and Applied.* London: John Allen, 1669.

McCoy, Charles S., and J. Wayne Baker. *Fountainhead of Federalism: Heinrich Bullinger and the Covenantal Tradition.* Louisville: Westminster John Knox, 1991.

McDermott, Gerald R. *Israel Matters: Why Christians Must Think Differently about the People and the Land.* Grand Rapids: Brazos, 2017.

McGrath, Alister E. *Thomas F. Torrance: An Intellectual Biography.* Edinburgh: T&T Clark, 1999.

Michael, Robert. "Antisemitism and the Church Fathers." In *Jewish-Christian Encounters over the Centuries: Symbiosis, Prejudice, Holocaust, Dialogue*, edited by Marvin Perry et al., 101–30. New York: Peter Lang, 1994.

Muller, Richard A. "Biblical Interpretation in the 16th & 17th Centuries." In *Historical Handbook of Major Biblical Interpreters*, edited by Donald K. McKim, 123–52. Downers Grove, IL: InterVarsity, 1998.

———. "Diversity in the Reformed Tradition: A Historiographical Introduction." In *Drawn into Controversie: Reformed Theological Diversity and Debates within Seventeenth-Century British Puritanism*, edited by Michael A. G. Haykin et al., 11–30. Göttingen: Vandenhoeck & Ruprecht, 2011.

———. *Post-Reformation Reformed Dogmatics*, vol. 2, Holy Scripture. Grand Rapids: Baker, 2003.

———. "Reception and Response: Referencing and Understanding Calvin in Seventeenth- Century Calvinism." In *Calvin and His Influence, 1509–2009*, edited by Irena Backus et al., 182–201. Oxford: Oxford University Press, 2011.

———. *The Unaccommodated Calvin: Studies in the Foundation of a Theological Tradition.* Oxford: Oxford University Press, 2001.

Murray, John. *The Epistle to the Romans.* Grand Rapids: Eerdmans, 1965.

Oberman, Heiko A. "John Calvin: The Mystery of His Impact." In *Calvin Studies VI*, edited by John H. Leith, 1–14. Richmond, VA: Union Theological Seminary, 1992.

———. *The Two Reformations: The Journey from the Last Days to the New World*, edited by Donald Weinstein. New Haven: Yale University Press.

Opitz, Peter. *Ulrich Zwingli: Prophet, Heretic, Pioneer of Protestantism*, translated by Rona Johnston. Eugene, OR: Cascade, 2024.

Owen, John. *The Works of John Owen*, vol. 4, edited by William H. Goold. Edinburgh: Banner of Truth, 1974.

———. *The Works of John Owen*, vol. 18, edited by William H. Goold. Edinburgh: Johnstone and Hunter, 1850–855.

Packer, James I. "John Calvin and Reformed Europe." In *Great Leaders of the Christian Church*, edited by John D. Woodbridge, 208–15. Chicago: Moody, 1989.

Pak, G. Sujin. "A Break with Anti-Judaic Exegesis: John Calvin and the Unity of the Testaments." *Calvin Theological Journal* 46, no. 1 (2011) 7–28.

———. "Calvin beyond Literal and Allegorical Reading: Calvin and Old Testament Metaphors." In *The Old Testament, Calvin and the Reformed Tradition*, edited by Yudha Thianto, 10–32. Leiden: Brill, 2024.

———. *The Judaizing Calvin: Sixteenth-Century Debates over the Messianic Psalms.* Oxford: Oxford University Press, 2010.

———. *The Reformation of Prophecy: Early Modern Interpretations of the Prophet and Old Testament Prophecy.* Oxford: Oxford University Press, 2018.

Parker, T. H. L. *John Calvin.* Tring, UK: Lion, 1975.

Pater, Calvin Augustine. "Calvin, the Jews and the Judaic Legacy." In *In Honor of John Calvin, 1509–64: Papers from the 1986 International Calvin Symposium, McGill University*, edited by Edward J. Furcha, 256–95. Montreal: FRS, McGill University, 1987.

Perkins, William. "Commentary on Galatians." In *The Works of William Perkins*, vol. 2, edited by Paul M. Smalley. Grand Rapids: Reformation Heritage, 2015.

Pitkin, Barbara. *Calvin, the Bible, and History: Exegesis and Historical Reflection in the Era of the Reformation.* Oxford: Oxford University Press, 2020.

Price, David H. *Johannes Reuchlin and the Campaign to Destroy Jewish Books.* Oxford: Oxford University Press, 2011.

Puckett, David L. *John Calvin's Exegesis of the Old Testament.* Louisville, KY: Westminster John Knox, 1995.

Robinson, Jack Hughes. *John Calvin and the Jews.* New York: Peter Lang, 1992.

Ryle, J. C. *Are You Ready for the End of Time? Understanding Future Events from Prophetic Passages of the Bible.* Fearn, UK: Christian Focus, 2001.

Schreiner, Susan. "Calvin as an Interpreter of Job." In *Calvin and the Bible*, edited by Donald K. McKim, 53–84. Cambridge: Cambridge University Press, 2006.

Schultz, Arnold. "Amos." In *Daniel and Minor Prophets with Wycliffe Bible Commentary*, edited by Charles F. Pfeiffer and Everett F. Harrison, 117–32. New York: Iversen-Norman Associates, 1975.

Schweitzer, Frederick M. "Medieval Perceptions of Jews and Judaism." In *Jewish-Christian Encounters over the Centuries: Symbiosis, Prejudice, Holocaust, Dialogue*, edited by Marvin Perry et al., 131–68. New York: Peter Lang, 1994.

Selderhuis, Herman. "Calvin, 1509–2009." In *Calvin and His Influence, 1509–2009*, edited by Irena Backus et al., 144–58. Oxford: Oxford University Press, 2011.

Shute, Dan. "*And All Israel Shall Be Saved*: Peter Martyr and John Calvin on the Jews according to Romans, Chapters 9, 10 and 11." In *Peter Martyr Vermigli and the European Reformation: Semper Reformanda*, edited by Frank A. James, 159–76. Leiden: Brill, 2004.

Sibbes, Richard. "The Bruised Reed and Smoking Flax." In *Works of Richard Sibbes*, vol.1, edited by Alexander B. Grosart, 33–101. Edinburgh: Banner of Truth, 1979.

Spencer, Stephen R. "Reformed Theology, Covenant Theology, and Dispensationalism," in *Integrity of Heart, Skillfulness of Hands*, ed. Charles H. Dyer et al., 238–54. Grand Rapids: Baker, 1994.

Steinmetz, David C. "John Calvin and the Jews: A Problem of Political Theology." *Political Theology* 10, no. 3 (2009) 391–409.

———. "John Calvin as an Interpreter of the Bible." In *Calvin and The Bible*, edited by Donald K. McKim, 282–91. Cambridge: Cambridge University Press, 2006.

Tertullian. "On Modesty." In *The Ante-Nicene Fathers*, vol. 4, edited by Alexander Roberts et al., 74–101. Edinburgh: T&T Clark, 1994.

Thompson, Bard. *Humanists and Reformers: A History of the Renaissance and Reformation*. Grand Rapids: Eerdmans, 1996.

Thompson, John L. "Calvin As a Biblical Interpreter." In *The Cambridge Companion to John Calvin*, edited by Donald K. McKim, 58–73. Cambridge: Cambridge University Press, 2004.

Toon, Peter. *Puritans, the Millennium and the Future of Israel: Puritan Eschatology 1600 to 1660*. Cambridge: James Clarke, 1970.

Torrance, David W. "Israel Today, in the Light of God's Word." In *The Witness of the Jews to God*, edited by David W. Torrance, 105–14. Edinburgh: Handsel, 1982.

———. *The Reluctant Minister: Memoirs by David W. Torrance*. Eugene, OR: Wipf & Stock, 2015.

———. "The Witness of the Jews to God (Their Purpose in History)." In *The Witness of the Jews to God*, edited by David W. Torrance, 1–12. Edinburgh: Handsel, 1982.

Torrance, David W., and George Taylor, *Israel, God's Servant: God's Key to the Redemption of the World*. London: Paternoster, 2007.

Torrance, Thomas F. "The Divine Vocation and Destiny of Israel in World History." In *The Witness of the Jews to God*, edited by David W. Torrance, 85–104. Edinburgh: Handsel, 1982.

———. *Incarnation: The Person and Life of Christ*, edited by Robert T. Walker. Downers Grove, IL: InterVarsity, 2008.

———. "Salvation Is of the Jews." *The Evangelical Quarterly* 22 (1950) 164–73.

Turretin, Francis. *Institutes of Elenctic Theology*, vol. 3. Translated by George Musgrave Giger. Phillipsburg, NJ: Presbyterian and Reformed, 1997.

VanGemeren, Willem A. "Israel as the Hermeneutical Crux in the Interpretation of Prophecy (II)." *Westminster Theological Journal* 46 (1984) 254–97.

Van Genderen, J., and W. H. Velema. *Concise Reformed Dogmatics*. Translated by Gerrit Bilkes and Ed M. van der Maas. Phillipsburg, NJ: Presbyterian and Reformed, 2008.

Van Ravenswaay, J. Marius J. Lange. "Calvin and the Jews." In *The Calvin Handbook*, edited by Herman J. Selderhuis, 143–46. Grand Rapids: Eerdmans, 2009.

Venema, Cornelis P. *The Promise of the Future.* Edinburgh: Banner of Truth, 2000.

Vos, Geerhardus. *Reformed Dogmatics.* Translated by Richard B. Gaffin. Bellingham, WA: Lexham, 2020.

Warfield, Benjamin B. "Calvin and the Reformation." In *Selected Shorter Writings of Benjamin B. Warfield–I*, 401–6, edited by John E. Meeter. Nutley, NJ: Presbyterian and Reformed, 1970.

Wendel, François. *Calvin: Origins and Development of His Religious Thought.* Translated by Philip Mairet. Grand Rapids: Baker, 1997.

Wilcox, Pete. "Calvin as Commentator on the Prophets." In *Calvin and the Bible*, edited by Donald K. McKim, 107–30. Cambridge: Cambridge University Press, 2006.

Witsius, Herman. *The Economy of the Covenants between God and Man*, vol. 2. Kingsburg, CA: Den Dulk Christian Foundation, 1990.

Zachman, Randall C. "Calvin as Commentator on Genesis." In *Calvin and the Bible*, edited by Donald K. McKim, 1–29. Cambridge: Cambridge University Press, 2006.

———. "John Calvin (1509–1564)." In *The Reformation Theologians*, edited by Carter Lindberg, 184–97. Oxford: Blackwell, 2002.

Subject Index

Abraham, 7–10
Abrahamic covenant, 19–22, 38,
    42–44, 71–72, 78
Alexandrian school, xxn36
allegorical exegesis, xx–xxi, 89–90,
    92–94
Alsted, Johann Heinrich, 30–31
anagogical, xxi
analogical reading, 31
antisemitism, 78–79
Armageddon, 36
Armstrong, Brian, xix–xx
Augustine, 59–60

Babylon, 73
Baille, Robert, 35
Barth, Karl, 13–15, 61
Bavinck, Herman, 13–14
Beeke, Joel, 85
Beza, Theodore, xvi, 74–75
biblical commentary, xviii–xix
biblical inspiration, 88
biblical languages, xvi–xvii, 58
Boice, James Montgomery, 33–34
Bomberg Hebrew Bible, 58
Bonar, Andrew, 77
Bouwsma, William, xixn32
Brakel, Wilhelmus à, 31, 34–35,
    81–82
Brueggemann, Walter, xin11, 88n1

Bucer, Martin, xii, 58, 74
Bullinger, Heinrich, 17, 46, 68
Burge, Gary, ixn1

Calvin, John, xv–xxii, 1–13, 15,
    17–23, 25–26, 28–32, 42–80,
    88–95
Capito, Wolfgang, xii, 30, 37, 76
Cauvin, Jean, xv
Chafer, Lewis Sperry, 4
Chapman, Colin, ixn1
chiliasm, 28n52, 30, 32, 35
Chrysostom, John, 62–63
Church of Scotland, 77n72
Collège de la Marche, xv
Collège de Montaigu, xv
Collège Royal, xvi
communion with God, xx
covenant of grace, 3, 9
covenant of salvation, 18

Davidic kingdom, 28–29, 35–36, 94
De Greef, Wulfert, x
Delitzsch, Franz, 24–25
dispensation, 26
divine grace, 7–9
divine revelation, 3

Edwards, Jonathan, 25n40, 82–83
election, 4, 7–10, 45–47

www.ingramcontent.com/pod-product-compliance
Lightning Source LLC
Chambersburg PA
CBHW070458090426
42735CB00012B/2604